Cicero (106–43 BCE) wa [illegible] id philosopher, widely regarded [illegible] s. A defender of the Republic a [illegible] on Greek philosophy to explore law, ethics, and political theory. His writings helped shape the foundations of Western political thought, natural law theory, and republican ideals.

R.J. Smith is an Australian essayist, novelist, translator, and academic living in France.

MAXIMA WESTERN CANON EDITIONS

The Epic of Gilgamesh
The Old Testament
The Iliad
The Odyssey
Oresteia
Medea
Histories
Oedipus Rex
History of the Peloponnesian War
Apology
Symposium
The Republic
Poetics
Ethics
Metaphysics
The Aeneid
Metamorphoses
Meditations
On the Republic
The New Testament
Confessions
The City of God
Beowulf
The Song of Roland
Summa Theologica
The Divine Comedy
The Decameron
The Canterbury Tales
Le Morte d'Arthur
In Praise of Folly
Utopia
The Prince
Institutes of the Christian Religion
Essays
The Faerie Queene
Hamlet
Macbeth
Don Quixote
Novum Organum
The Rights of War and Peace
Two Chief World Systems
Discourse on Method
Leviathan
Tartuffe
Paradise Lost
Pensées
Ethics (Spinoza)
The Pilgrim's Progress
Discourse on Metaphysics
A Letter Concerning Toleration

Two Treatises of Government

Gulliver's Travels

A Treatise of Human Nature

The Spirit of the Laws

Second Discourse

Candide

The Social Contract

The Wealth of Nations

Critique of Pure Reason

The Federalist Papers

Principles of Morals and Legislation

Reflections on Revolution in France

The Rights of Man

Vindication of the Rights of Woman

Phenomenology of Spirit

Faust

Pride and Prejudice

Frankenstein

The World as Will and Representation

The Red and the Black

General View of Positivism

Democracy in America

Père Goriot

Hero-Worship

Dead Souls

The Communist Manifesto

Moby-Dick

Madame Bovary

Les Fleurs du Mal

On Liberty

On the Origin of Species

Great Expectations

Les Misérables

Crime and Punishment

War and Peace

Middlemarch

A Doll's House

The Brothers Karamazov

Thus Spoke Zarathustra

Beyond Good and Evil

The Golden Bough

The Interpretation of Dreams

Protestant Ethic & Spirit of Capitalism

In Search of Lost Time

The Metamorphosis

The Decline of the West

Tractatus Logico-Philosophicus

The Waste Land

Ulysses

Mrs. Dalloway

MAXIMA PRESS

KNOW MORE

On the Republic

(*trans. George William Featherstonhaugh*)

and

On the Laws

(*trans. Francis F. Barham*)

by Cicero

On the Republic, translated by George William Featherstonhaugh, was first published in 1841. *On the Laws*, translated by Francis F. Barham, was first published in 1853.

ISBN: 978-2-487992-65-8.

Contents

Introduction

In the great tradition of Western political thought, the writings of Marcus Tullius Cicero occupy a place of enduring relevance. A statesman, orator, philosopher, and patriot, Cicero sought not merely to analyze politics in the abstract, but to articulate a vision of justice grounded in human nature, practical governance, and the ethical obligations of citizenship. In *On the Republic* and *On the Laws*, Cicero attempts one of the most ambitious philosophical syntheses of the ancient world: to adapt the lofty ideals of Greek philosophy to the real-world challenges of the Roman Republic.

This volume brings together two of Cicero's most influential philosophical dialogues, translated respectively by George William Featherstonhaugh (*On the Republic*) and Francis F. Barham (*On the Laws*). Written in the tumultuous final decades of the Roman Republic, these works offer both a defense of republican institutions and a deeply moral framework for public life. Through imagined dialogues between Roman statesmen, Cicero explores the nature of justice, the role of law, the importance of mixed government, and the responsibilities of rulers and citizens alike.

Although these works are fragmentary—especially *On the Republic*, of which only portions survive—their intellectual legacy is vast. Cicero's synthesis of Stoic ethics, Platonic political theory, and Roman pragmatism laid a foundation that would shape the development of political thought from antiquity through the Enlightenment to the present day.

Historical Background

Born in 106 BCE in Arpinum, a provincial town southeast of Rome, Cicero rose through the *cursus honorum*—the sequential offices of Roman public service—at a time of great instability. His lifetime witnessed the erosion of republican norms, the violent rivalry of powerful generals, and the slow, relentless collapse of the Roman Republic.

By the time Cicero composed *On the Republic* (written around 54–51 BCE) and *On the Laws* (circa 52–51 BCE), Rome had already endured decades of social upheaval. The reform movements of the Gracchi brothers in the late second century BCE had revealed the deep fault lines between Rome's aristocratic elite and its disenfranchised masses. Subsequent years saw the rise of demagogues, the corruption of electoral politics, and the increasing reliance on military force to resolve political disputes.

Cicero, a *novus homo* (or "new man") with no noble lineage, distinguished himself through eloquence and intellect, becoming consul in 63 BCE—a rare feat for someone of his background. His career was marked by a fervent defense of republican ideals, most famously in his opposition to Catiline's conspiracy, which he denounced in a series of orations that exemplify his belief in the rule of law and civic virtue.

Yet even as Cicero defended the Republic, its foundations were eroding. The political rivalry between Julius Caesar and Pompey, the First Triumvirate's domination of Roman politics, and the eventual outbreak of civil war rendered the old republican structures increasingly obsolete.

Cicero, often caught between competing powers, was exiled, recalled, and ultimately marginalized during Caesar's rise. He continued to write and advocate for constitutional government, but the tide of history was against him. In 43 BCE, during the proscriptions of the Second Triumvirate, Cicero was assassinated—a martyr for the cause of liberty, as later generations would remember him.

On the Republic and *On the Laws* were written as part of Cicero's philosophical retreat during these tumultuous years, when he sought to articulate in dialogue form a vision of what a just and stable republic ought to be. Drawing on the Platonic model of philosophical dialogue, he cast prominent Roman statesmen—Scipio Aemilianus, Laelius, and others—as interlocutors in debates about the ideal state. Yet unlike Plato, Cicero grounded his dialogues in Roman experience and law.

These works represent his belief that philosophy could be brought into service of the state, that wisdom and virtue could illuminate the path through chaos. In composing these dialogues,

Cicero hoped not only to preserve Rome's traditions but to renew them.

Key Themes

For Cicero, justice is not a human invention or a matter of custom, but a feature of the natural order. Drawing on Stoic and Platonic thought, he argues that there exists a universal, rational law—*lex naturae*—that binds all human beings by virtue of their shared reason. The true state is one that conforms to this natural law, promoting the common good rather than the interests of the powerful few.

In *On the Republic*, Cicero articulates a theory of mixed government, in which the best features of monarchy, aristocracy, and democracy are combined to create a stable and just political order. He praises the Roman constitution for achieving this balance, with consuls representing monarchy, the Senate representing aristocracy, and the popular assemblies embodying democratic participation. This vision reflects Cicero's admiration for the Roman Republic at its best, but also his awareness of its fragility. Stability, he argues, depends not only on institutions but on the virtue of its citizens and leaders.

Cicero insists that the health of the republic depends on the moral character of its people. Public service is not a matter of ambition or self-enrichment but a moral duty. The ideal statesman, modeled in figures like Scipio Aemilianus, is wise, just, and guided by reason. Cicero's political philosophy is thus deeply ethical: politics is not separate from philosophy but its practical application.

On the Laws continues this ethical-political project by exploring the foundations of law itself. For Cicero, all positive human laws must be grounded in the higher law of nature. If a law violates justice, it is not truly a law at all—a radical assertion with enduring implications. The dialogue proposes a constitution based on Roman institutions but guided by philosophical principles: moderation, separation of powers, checks and balances, and moral education.

Religion also plays a significant role in Cicero's thought. Unlike many modern political theorists, he does not separate religion from public life. Instead, he sees religious observance as a means of reinforcing moral behavior and social cohesion. Yet his approach is more philosophical than theological; he emphasizes reverence for divine reason rather than blind obedience to superstition.

Significance to the Western Canon

Cicero's synthesis of Greek philosophy with Roman political practice provided a bridge between two intellectual worlds and helped shape the moral and political vocabulary of the Roman Empire.

But it was in later centuries, especially during the Renaissance and Enlightenment, that Cicero's stature reached its peak. Renaissance humanists revered him as the ideal orator and philosopher, a man who embodied the fusion of wisdom and action. Petrarch, Erasmus, and Thomas More all drew inspiration from Cicero's writings, seeing in him a guide for the moral renewal of society through education, virtue, and republican government.

During the early modern period, Cicero's political philosophy became a foundational source for thinkers grappling with questions of sovereignty, liberty, and the rule of law. John Locke cited him as a moral authority, and Montesquieu's theory of the separation of powers owes much to Cicero's reflections on mixed government.

In the American founding, Cicero's ideas were central: the framers of the U.S. Constitution drew on his writings when articulating republican ideals, natural rights, and the need for virtuous leadership. John Adams referred to Cicero as "the great master of eloquence and philosophy," and Thomas Jefferson included his works in recommended reading for young statesmen.

Cicero's conception of natural law, in particular, has had an enduring impact on legal theory. His claim that unjust laws are not true laws helped lay the groundwork for resistance to tyranny and the defense of universal human rights. From the anti-absolutist writings of the seventeenth century to the legal arguments of the twentieth-century civil rights movement, Cicero's moral jurisprudence has remained a touchstone for those who see law as a servant of justice, not merely power.

Even in literary terms, Cicero has left his mark. His elegant Latin style influenced countless writers, and his philosophical dialogues provided a model for intellectual inquiry that combines rigor with accessibility. His personal courage in defending the Republic, even in the face of death, has inspired generations to see politics not as a game of power but as a moral endeavor.

On the Republic and *On the Laws* speak to the perennial challenges of human society: how to govern justly, how to reconcile liberty with order, how to live ethically in a world of compromise and conflict. Though written in the dying days of the Roman Republic, they are infused with hope—the hope that reason, virtue, and law can prevail over ambition and chaos.

The translations by George William Featherstonhaugh and Francis F. Barham continue to serve as valuable conduits between ancient wisdom and modern inquiry.

In returning to these works, we engage not only with the past but with the fundamental questions that continue to animate political life. Cicero invites us to imagine a better republic—not merely in form, but in spirit. He reminds us that politics, at its best, is the art of serving the common good through reasoned deliberation, moral courage, and a steadfast commitment to justice.

As republics around the world face challenges both old and new, Cicero's voice resounds with undiminished clarity: the fate of a nation rests not merely in its laws or leaders, but in the character of its citizens and the principles they uphold. His works remain an indispensable part of our shared intellectual heritage—a legacy of thought, word, and action that continues to inspire the pursuit of a just and rules-based society.

R.J. Smith
Paris, 2025

ON THE REPUBLIC

BOOK I.

I. For without the strong feeling of patriotism, neither had G. Duelius, Aulus Atilius or L. Metellus freed us from the terror of Carthage; or the two Scipios extinguished with their blood the rising flame of the second punic war. Quintus Maximus would not have weakened, nor M. Marcellus have crushed the one which was springing up with still greater strength: or P. Africanus turning it from the gates of this city, have borne it amid the walls of our enemies. Yet it was not thought unbecoming in M. Cato, an unknown and a new man, by whom all of us who emulate his course are led as a bright example of industry and virtue, to enjoy the repose of Tusculum, that healthy and convenient situation. That insane man, however, as some have considered him, preferred when urged by no necessity, to contend amid those waves and tempests to extreme old age; rather than pass his days in the most agreeable manner, amid so much ease and tranquillity. Men without number I omit, each of whom were benefactors to the State, and who are not far removed from the remembrance of this generation. I forbear to commemorate them, lest any one should reproach me with neglecting to speak of himself or his immediate friends. This one truth I would mark, that nature has so strongly implanted in man the necessity of virtue, and so powerful an inclination to defend the common welfare, that this principle overcomes all the blandishments of voluptuousness and ease.

II. Yet to possess virtue, like some art, without exercising it, is insufficient. Art indeed, when not effective, is still comprehended in science. The efficacy of all virtue consists in its use. Its greatest end is the government of states, and the perfection not in words but in deeds, of those very things which are taught in the halls. For nothing is propounded by philosophers, concerning what is esteemed to be just and proper, that is not confirmed and assured by those who have legislated for states. For from whence springs piety, or from whom religion? Whence the law, either of nations, or that which is called civil? Whence justice, faith, equity? Whence modesty, continence, the dread of turpitude, the love of praise and esteem? Whence fortitude in trouble and dangers? From those who having laid a foundation for these things in early education, have strengthened some of them by the influence of manners, and sanctioned others by the influence of laws. Of Xenocrates, one of the noblest of philosophers, it is said, that when he was asked what his disciples learnt of him, he replied "to do that of their own choice, which the laws enjoined them to do," therefore the citizen who obliges every one by the authority and fear of the law to do that, which philosophers by reasoning, with difficulty persuade a few to do, is to be preferred to those learned men who only dispute about these things. For which of their orations, however exquisite, can be compared in value to a well constituted state, to public right and to morals. Truly as great and powerful cities, as Ennius says, are as I think, to be preferred to villages and castles; so those who stand pre-eminent in those cities, in authority and counsel, are to be esteemed far before those in wisdom, who are altogether ignorant of the conduct of public affairs. And since we are chiefly urged by a desire to increase the possessions of the human race, and seek by our counsels and labours, to surround the life of man with gratification and security, and are incited by the instincts of nature to these enjoyments; let us hold the course which was always that of the best men: nor attend to those signals which speculative philosophers make from their retirement, to allure back those who are already far advanced.

III. Against these reasons so certain and so clear, it is urged by those who are opposed to us: first, the labour to be undergone in preserving the public welfare; a slight impediment to the zealous and industrious, not alone in matters of such high import, but in inferior things: whether in studies or in official stations; and to be despised even in affairs of business. To this they add the dangers to which life is exposed, and the dread of death, which brave men scorn; being wont to view it as more wretched to waste away by infirmity and old age, than to seize an occasion to devote that life to the advantage of their country, which one day must be rendered to nature. It is here however they deem themselves most successful and eloquent, when they bring forward the calamities of eminent men, and the injuries heaped upon them by their ungrateful countrymen. Here come the instances in Grecian history. Miltiades, the conqueror and subduer of the Persians, with those wounds yet streaming, which he received in front, in the height of victory: preserved from the weapons of the enemy, to waste away his life in the chains of his countrymen. And Themistocles proscribed and driven from the country he had freed, flying, not to the harbours of that Greece he had preserved, but to the barbarous shores he had harrassed. Nor indeed are instances wanting among the Athenians of levity and cruelty towards great numbers of their citizens; instances which springing up repeatedly among them, are said also to have abounded too conspicuously in our city. For either the exile of Camillus, the misfortune of Ahala, the ill will towards Nasica, or the expulsion of Lenas, or the condemnation of Opimus is remembered: or the flight of Metellus, the sad overthrow of C. Marius, the cutting off of the most eminent citizens, or the destruction of many of them, which soon after followed. Nor indeed is my name forgotten. And I judge that deeming themselves to owe both life and ease to my peril and counsel, they have a more deep and tender remembrance of me. But it is not easy to explain how they who cross the seas for the sake of observing or describing * * *

[Two pages wanting.]

IV. * * * * At the expiration of my consulship, when in the assembly of the Roman people, I swore that the republic had been saved by my exertions, which they confirmed by universal acclamation, I was requited for the cares and vexations of every injury. Albeit my reverses had more honour than pain attached to them, and less disquietude than glory. Greater was my pleasure at receiving the approbation of good men, than my regret at observing the satisfaction of the bad. But had it happened otherwise, as I said, what complaint could I make? Nothing unforeseen could have occurred, nor more grievous than I might have expected for so many of my deeds. For I was one who could well have gathered greater fruits from ease than others, on account of the agreeable variety of the studies I had pursued from my childhood; and if any disaster had overtaken the republic, I need not have sustained a greater share of it, but have divided it equally with the rest. I hesitated not to oppose myself to those stormy tempests, and almost raging waves, for the sake of preserving my fellow citizens, and of accomplishing at my own risk the common safety of all. For our country has not produced us, or educated us under a law, that she is entitled to no support on our part, lending herself as it were to our convenience only; furnishing a secure refuge, and a tranquil and peaceful asylum to our indolence: but rather holds as pledges to her, to be employed for her benefit, the many and great faculties of our mind, genius, and reason; and only permits us to appropriate to our private purposes, that portion of them, of which she stands in no need.

V. The pretences which are urged for the enjoyment of indolence are not to be listened to. As when it is stated that the public affairs are meddled with by men worthy of no confidence, with whom it is disgraceful to associate: yet to contend against whom is a miserable and dangerous effort, especially when the multitude is excited. For which reason a prudent man ought not to take the reins, when he is not able to restrain the mad and untameable violence of the vulgar: or a generous man expose himself to the lashes of contumely in a strife with low and outrageous adversaries: or a wise man hope to withdraw from such a contest without injury. As if there could well be a more just cause for good and firm men, endowed with noble minds, to stand forth in aid of their country, than that they may not be subject to bad men; nor suffer the republic to be lacerated by them, before the desire of saving it may come too late.

VI. But who can approve of their exception, that a wise man ought not to take upon him any part of the public affairs, unless an occasion of extraordinary need should drive him to it? as if indeed a greater necessity could ever have happened to any one, than occurred to myself. How could I have been useful then, had I not been consul? and how could I have been consul, had I not pursued that course of life from my youth, which belonging to the equestrian rank, in which I was born, enabled me to attain the first honours of the state? No man therefore can assume at pleasure the ability of aiding in the public service, however urgent the danger may be, unless he stands in that relation to his country, which fits him for the occasion. And it appears to me most marvellous, that in the discourse of learned men, they who declare themselves unable to steer in a calm sea, because they have never been taught, nor have ever studied the subject, talk of taking the helm in the midst of the greatest storms. For these very men openly declare, and pride themselves greatly upon it, that they have never studied or taught the mode of establishing or protecting the public interest; which they think the exclusive province, not of learned and erudite men, but of those who are practised in these matters. What consistency is there then in promising to aid the republic in times of peril, when they are incapable of the easier task of directing it in the calmest moments? And although, in truth, the philosopher is not wont of his own accord, to consider the details of state affairs, unless called upon by the times to do it, when indeed he will not decline what duty imposes on him; nevertheless, I judge the knowledge of state affairs is least to be neglected by a wise man; that every thing may be familiar to him, for he cannot tell the moment, when it may be necessary for him to avail himself of his knowledge.

VII. These things I have somewhat enlarged upon, because the discussion proposed and undertaken by me in this work, was on government: and in order to prevent its being without effect, it was necessary in the first instance, to remove every doubt as to the duty of engaging in the public service. Nevertheless if there are any who are governed by the opinions of philosophers, let them turn their attention for a while, and listen to those who enjoy a proud pre-eminence among learned men, even when they have not borne any charge in the republic; still whom I deem from the extent of their studies, and their writings on government, to have been invested with functions appertaining to the public interest. But those seven, whom the Greeks call wise, I perceive have almost all been greatly engaged in public affairs. For there is no one thing in which human worth is more nearly allied to the power of the gods, than to found new states, or to preserve those already founded.

VIII. Concerning which matters, since it hath happened to me, to be deemed something worthy of memory in my administration of public affairs, and to possess some talent for unfolding them; not only in practice, but being versed too in the art of speaking and teaching: while of those before me, some were perfect in debate, yet unknown by their deeds; others of respectable parts for business, without the talent of oratory. Still it is not my intention here to bring forward any new system invented by myself, but to repeat a discussion, that took place at a certain period of our history, among our most illustrious and wise men, which was related to me a long time ago in my youth, by P. Rutilius Rufus, when we were at Smyrna together: in the which I think scarce any point was omitted that belongs to the consideration of these great matters.

IX. When P. Africanus, the son of Paulus, established Latin holidays in his gardens, during the consulate of Tuditanus, and Aquilius; and his most intimate friends had promised to visit him frequently at that season. On the morning of the first day, Q. Tubero, the eldest son of his sister, came. Pleased with his visit, and kindly addressing him "What! Tubero," said he, "is it you so early? I should have thought these holidays would have given you a favourable opportunity of pursuing your literary inquiries." "Why in truth," replied he, "I can apply all my leisure to my books, for they are always disengaged. But to find you at leisure, is very remarkable; especially at this time so critical for the republic." "So help me Hercules," said Scipio, "however you find me, it is more idle in appearance than in truth." "You must now," said Tubero, "relax your mind a little also, for several of us have determined if it is not inconvenient to you, to spend some of our leisure with you." "With all my heart," replied Scipio, "provided we may acquire some information thereby on philosophical subjects."

X. "Since you invite and encourage me to it yourself," said Tubero, "let us first converse, Africanus, before the others come, about the meaning of this double sun which has been spoken of in the senate. For those who declare that they have seen two suns, are neither few in number, nor insignificant persons: so that it appears to be of less importance to doubt the fact, than to inquire into the cause of it." "Would that we had with us our excellent Panætius," said Scipio, "who among other objects of knowledge, was so diligent an inquirer about celestial phenomena. As to myself, Tubero—for to you I will freely declare what I think; I am not drawn in to adopt in matters of this sort, the opinions of our friend, who pronounces things which are scarcely within the reach of conjecture, to be as manifest, as if he beheld them with his eyes, or could lay his hands upon them. On which account I am accustomed to consider Socrates much wiser, who leaves the consideration of such things aside, and teaches that the phenomena about which nature may be interrogated, are either beyond the force of human reason, or irrelevant to the conduct of human affairs." "I know not," rejoined Tubero, "what authority there is for the fact, that Socrates rejected all discussion upon such matters, and confined himself to the moral conduct of human life. For what author is to be commended, as more ample on that head than Plato; in whose writings, in many places, it is the custom of Socrates in discussing morals, the virtues, and finally public affairs; to allude studiously to the science of numbers, to geometry, and to harmony, after the Pythagorean mode." Scipio answered, "these things are as you say; but I dare say you have heard, Tubero, that Plato after the death of Socrates, was carried by the love of knowledge first into Egypt, afterwards into Italy and Sicily, that he might obtain an insight into the discoveries of Pythagoras. That he associated much with Archytas the Tarentine, and with Timæus of Locram. That he acquired the commentaries of Philolaus, and perceiving that the name of Pythagoras was at that time in great reputation in those places, he dedicated his time to the disciples of Pythagoras and to their opinions. But as he had loved Socrates alone, and wished to make all things conducive to his reputation, he interwove very skilfully the subtlety and humour of the Socratic style with the mysteries of Pythagoras, and with many branches of the arts."

As Scipio ceased to speak, he suddenly saw L. Furius approaching, and as soon as he had kindly saluted him, he took him by the hand, and placed him on his couch. And as P. Rutilius the accomplished preserver of this conversation appeared at the same time, saluting him also in the same manner, he bade him be seated near to Tubero. "What are you engaged in," said Furius; "hath our arrival broken in upon your conversation?" "Not in the least," replied Africanus, "for it is precisely about matters, such as Tubero has just been introducing, that thou art wont diligently to inquire into, and to investigate. And indeed our friend Rutilius was in the habit occasionally of discussing things of this kind with me, when we were under the walls of Numantia." "What is the subject you have fallen upon?" said Philus. "These two suns," replied he, "respecting which I am desirous of hearing your opinion."

XII. As he spoke this, a boy announced that Lælius was approaching, having already left his house; upon which Scipio having dressed himself, left his chamber, and had made but a few paces in the portico, when he saluted Lælius who was approaching, and those who were with him: Spurius Mummius, to whom he was particularly attached; Fannius, and Quintus Scævola, sons-in-law of Lælius, highly gifted young men of the quæstorial age. And having welcomed them all, he made another turn on the portico, placing Lælius in the middle; for in their friendship it was a sort of law between them, that Lælius did homage to Scipio as to a god, on account of his glorious pre-eminence in war; while in his turn Scipio, in private life, paid to Lælius all the reverence due to a parent, on account of his superior years. And having chatted a little together in various places, Scipio, who was very much enlivened and gratified with their arrival, was pleased to have them seated in a sunny place in a little meadow, on account of its being the winter season; which as they were about to do, M. Manilius came, a prudent and agreeable person, and very dear to them all; who being cordially saluted by Scipio and the rest, took his seat next to Lælius.

XIII. "It does not seem to me necessary," said Philus "that we should seek another subject of conversation on account of those who are arrived, but that we should observe more accuracy, and say something worthy of their ears." "What subject were you upon," said Lælius, "and what discussion are we come to be present at?" "Scipio was inquiring of me," replied Philus, "what my opinion was respecting the fact of two suns having been seen."

Lælius. "Why truly Philus, is there no longer any thing left for us to inquire about, touching our own domestic affairs, or those appertaining to the republic, that we must be exploring the things that are passing in the heavens?" "Dost thou then think," replied he, "that it does not concern our own mansions, to know what is passing, and what is done in that vast one, not the one surrounded by our walls, but that which constitutes the universe, and which the gods have given to us for a domicile, and a common country with themselves. Especially when if we are ignorant of them, many and very high matters will be hidden from us. As to myself, the contemplation and knowledge of these things delight me, as certainly as it does you, Lælius, and all who are eager in the pursuit of knowledge." "I offer no impediment," said Lælius, especially at this holiday time; but shall we hear any thing, or are we come too late?"

Philus. "Nothing has been discussed yet, and as the subject is entire, I freely concede to you, Lælius, the right of expressing your sentiments first."

Lælius. "Let us rather hear you, unless Manilius thinks, that some decree by way of compromise between these two suns may be adjusted; so that each may keep possession of its own part of the firmament." "You love still to banter that science, Lælius, in which I am proud to excel," replied Manilius, "and without which no one could know his own possession from anothers. But of that by and by. Let us now listen to Philus, who I perceive has a case of greater difficulty referred to him, than ever came before me or P. Mucius."

XIV. "I shall lay nothing new before you," said Philus, "nor any thing discovered or thought of by myself. I remember, however, that C. Sulpicius Gallus, a very learned man as you know; when this same phenomenon was stated to have been seen, being by chance in the house of M. Marcellus, who had been in the consulate with him; ordered a sphere to be placed before him, which the ancestor of M. Marcellus had taken from the conquered Syracusans, and brought out of their wealthy and embellished city; the only thing he had possessed himself of among so great a spoil. I had heard a great deal of this sphere, on account of the fame of Archimedes, but did not admire the construction of it so much; for another which Archimedes also had made, and which the same Marcellus had placed in the temple of virtue, was more elegant and remarkable in the general opinion. But subsequently, when Gallus began very scientifically to explain the nature of the mechanism; the Sicilian appeared to me to possess more genius, than human nature would seem to be capable of. Gallus said, that the other solid and full sphere was an old invention, and was first wrought by Thales of Miletas: but afterwards was delineated over with the fixed stars in the heavens by Eudoxus, the Cnidian, a disciple of Plato. The which adorned and embellished as it was by Eudoxus, Aratus who had no knowledge of astronomy, but a certain poetical faculty, many years afterwards extolled in his verses. The mechanism of this sphere, however, on which the motions of the sun, moon, and those five stars which are called wandering and irregular, are shown; could not be illustrated on that solid sphere.

But what appeared very admirable in this invention of Archimedes was, that he had discovered a method of producing the unequal and various courses, with their dissimilar velocities, by one revolution. When Gallus put this sphere in motion, the moon was made to succeed the sun by as many revolutions of the brass circle, as it actually took days to do in the heavens. From which the same setting of the sun was produced on the sphere as in the heavens: and the moon fell on the very point, where it met the shadow of the earth, when the sun from the region * * * *

[About ten pages wanting.]

XV. * * * * * for he was a man I was very much attached to, and I know that my father Paulus esteemed and placed the highest value on him. I remember when I was but a boy, being with my father, who was then consul in Macedonia; that while we were encamped, our army was struck with a religious dread, because the full and splendid moon in the serenity of the night, was suddenly eclipsed. He being then our lieutenant, the year just before that in which he was declared consul, did not hesitate the following day, to pronounce openly in the camp, that it was no prodigy. And that what had then taken place, would always occur in future at those particular periods, when the position of the sun was such, that its rays could not fall upon the moon. "But how could he," asked Tubero, "make men half wild, comprehend such matters, or venture to speak of them before the unenlightened?"

Scipio. "Indeed he did, and with great * * * *

[About two pages wanting.]

* * * * * there was neither a haughty ostentation, nor any thing in his speech unbecoming a grave personage; and he accomplished a point of great importance, in removing from the disturbed minds of the men, the influence of an idle and fearful superstition.

XVI. There was an occurrence similar to this during the great war, which the Athenians and Lacedemonians waged against each other with so much inveteracy. Darkness being suddenly produced by the obscuration of the sun, and a prodigious fear taking possession of the minds of the Athenians. Pericles, the first man in the city, in authority, in eloquence, and in council; taught the citizens what he had himself learnt from Anaxagoras, whose pupil he had been: that it was an unavoidable appearance at the particular period, when the moon had placed herself immediately before the orb of the sun: and although it did not take place every lunar period; it could nevertheless be occasioned only by the moon's motion. Having convinced them by reasoning, he delivered the people from their apprehension. For it was then a strange and unknown reason to give for an eclipse, that the sun and moon were in opposition to each other, which it is said, was first observed by Thales the Milesian. At a later period, this had not escaped our Ennius, who wrote about the year 350 of the building of Rome, in the nones of June; that "*the moon and night stood before the sun*." So great, however, is the advancement of knowledge in these matters, that from this day, which we find noted in the principal annals, and by Ennius; the previous occultations of the sun are fixed up to that which took place in the reign of Romulus, in the nones of the fifth month. During which darkness, Romulus, whom the laws of nature indeed would have carried to the tomb, is said to have been borne by his virtue to heaven.

XVII. Then Tubero, "Dost thou not perceive Africanus, that what appeared otherwise to thee a while ago * * * * * *

[About two pages wanting.]

* * * * * * "Who can perceive any grandeur in human affairs, whose eyes are accustomed to survey the empire of the gods? What are temporal things in the eyes of those conversant with eternal ones? What is there glorious to the contemplation of him, who looks at the small size of the earth; first as to its whole extent, then to that part of it which men inhabit? And yet we, confined to so small a portion of it, unknown to most nations, hope our name will be diffused to its utmost limits. What are lands, and houses, and flocks, and immense masses of gold and silver to him who neither considers them desirable nor calls them so: the fruition of which appears to him trifling, the use unsatisfactory, the possession uncertain: and which are often in the hands of the most contemptible of men? How fortunate may that man be esteemed, who alone claims a share in all things, not as the privilege of a

citizen, but of a philosopher: not by civil rights, but by the common law of nature, which forbids any one to be the proprietor of aught, of the proper use of which he is ignorant! Who considers our consulships and high offices, not to be sought after for the sake of personal advantage or glory; not as things to be coveted, but to be undertaken as duties. The man finally who can say that of himself which my ancestor Africanus, as Cato writes, was wont to say, "that he never was more busy than when he was doing nothing; and that he never was less alone, than when nobody was with him."

For who can deem Dionysius to have accomplished a greater thing, when by the greatest exertion he snatched their liberties from the citizens, than Archimedes his countryman, who appearing to be occupied in nothing, produced this sphere of which we were but now conversing? Are they not more alone, who find no one in the forum or in the crowd who chooses to talk with them, than those who without any witness can converse with themselves; or as it were, be present at the councils of the most learned men, when they solace themselves with their discoveries and writings? Who in truth can imagine any one to be more rich, than the man who has no wants, beyond the simple calls of nature; or more powerful than him, who has attained the possession of al that he desires; or more blessed than him who is freed from all anxiety of mind? or what man's fortune is better established than his, who can carry along with him, or out of a shipwreck as men are wont to say, all his possessions? What command, what office, what kingdom can be preferred to that condition of mind, which looking down upon all things human, and esteeming them to be the objects of an inferior wisdom, turns ever to the contemplation of those things that are divine and eternal: persuaded that they only deserve to be called men, who are refined by the sciences of humanity? That which has been said of Plato, or of some other sage, appears to me therefore very excellent. Who being borne by a tempest to unknown lands, and cast on a desert shore, while his companions were apprehensive on account of their ignorance of the place, is said to have perceived geometrical figures described on the sand. Which when he saw, he bade them all be of good heart, for he had seen vestiges of men. Not that he judged so from the cultivation of the fields which he beheld, but from these indications of science. For all these reasons, Tubero, learning, and learned men, and these thy studies have always been pleasing to me.

XVIII. Then said Lælius, "I am not bold enough, Scipio, to speak of these things: nor even to thee, or Philus, or Manilius * * * * *

[Two pages wanting]

* * * * in his paternal house we have had a friend, worthy to be imitated by him.

"Ælius Sextus, conspicuously discreet and wise." That he was conspicuously discreet and wise, is said by Ennius, not because he sought after what he was not able to discover, but because he answered those who made inquiries of him, in a manner to solve their difficulties and anxieties, in whose mouth when arguing against the studies of Gallus, were always these words of Achilles, in Iphigenia.

"Astrology, its signs; how are they read in heaven?
When goat or scorpion, or ferocious names arise,
The obvious earth is shunned, to scrutinize the skies."

He also said, for many times and willingly I listened to him, that Zethus the author of Pacuvius, was too great an enemy to science. The Neoptolemus of Ennius pleased him more; who says that he likes to philosophize but only with a few; not willing to give himself up to it altogether. But if the studies of the Greeks delight you so much, there are others freer and more easily diffused, which we may bring to the use of life, or even to that of the republic. As for these arts, their value consists, if in any thing, in stimulating and sharpening the genius of young boys; enabling them in this manner the better to comprehend greater things.

XIX. "I do not dissent from you, Lælius," said Tubero, "but ask what you understand by greater things?"

Lælius. "I will tell you in good faith, although you may somewhat despise me for it; since it is you who are asking Scipio about these celestial matters. As for myself, I think those things most worthy of our attention, which lay immediately before our eyes. How can it interest me that the grandson of L. Paulus by the mother's side, born of such a noble and illustrious family in this republic, should seek for reasons why two suns have been seen, when he does not inquire the cause why two senates, and almost two people exist in one republic? For as you perceive the death of Tiberius Gracchus, and even before that event, the whole proceedings of his tribunate were dividing one people into two parties: those who are the detractors of Scipio also, and are envious of him, urged on at first by P. Crassus and Appius Claudius, keep up notwithstanding their death, an opposition to us in the senate, through the influence of Metellus and P. Mucius. Nor will they suffer him to come forward, who is alone equal to so dangerous a crisis, amidst the factious and dangerous associations made under the Roman name: amidst violated compacts, and the new matters daily stirring by the seditious triumvirs, to the consternation of good and respectable men. Wherefore young men, if you will listen to me, entertain no apprehensions about this double sun: for either it is nothing at all, or if it is a reality, as far as it has been observed, there is nothing injurious in it. Either we can know nothing about such matters, or even if we could know all about them, we should not be better or happier for that knowledge. But one senate and one people we may have; that is practicable. And if it is not done, we shall suffer for it. And we know it is otherwise, and that if it were effected, we should have more stability, and be happier and better."

XX. Then Mucius. "What is it we have to learn, in your opinion, Lælius, that we may be able to effect what you require of us?"

Lælius. "Those sciences whose tendency is to enable us to be useful to the state; for I deem that to be the most pre-eminent gift of wisdom, as well as the noblest fruit of virtue and duty. Wherefore that these holidays may be productive of conversations in an especial manner useful to the republic, let us entreat Scipio to impart to us, what he deems to be the happiest condition of a state. Afterwards we can consider other matters, the knowledge of which I hope will bring us to the subject before us, and will unfold the causes of the present condition of things.

[Two pages wanting.]

XXI. * * * * * not for that cause alone I wished it, but because I thought it proper that the first person in the republic should first speak on public affairs; and because I remembered that you were accustomed frequently to discuss with Panætius before Polybius, two Greeks extremely versed in civil affairs; and that you had proved by various reasonings the excellence of that form of government, which our ancestors had transmitted to us from so distant a period. In the which matter, you, being more competent to it, will do an agreeable thing to us all, (for I speak also for the rest,) if you will unfold to us your opinion of the commonwealth."

XXII. "I cannot," he began, "say that I have been in the habit of turning my mind more intensely and diligently to the consideration of any subject, than the very one which you now propose to me, Lælius. For when I perceive that every artificer who truly excels in his vocation, is filled with anxiety, care, and zeal, lest any one should surpass him in his art. I, whose chief duty, bequeathed to me by my parents and ancestors, is the conduct and administration of the republic, must confess myself more indolent than any artisan, if I bestowed less attention on the greatest of arts, than he does on the most insignificant. But neither am I satisfied with the writings on this subject which the first and wisest among the Greeks have left to us; while I hesitate to establish my own conclusions in preference to theirs. Wherefore I intreat you, not to listen to me as one entirely ignorant of the affairs of the Greeks, nor as one who gives them the preference to our own writers, particularly in matters of this kind; but as one liberally brought up by the diligence of distinguished parents, and ardent in the love of knowledge from his youth; yet nevertheless much more formed by domestic experience, than by literary studies."

XXIII. "I doubt," said Philus here, "whether any one has ever excelled you in genius. We know to what studies you have always been partial, and that in your acquaintance with the great affairs of the state, you have surpassed every one: wherefore if as you say, your mind has been particularly turned to matters which have now become almost a science: I feel very much indebted to Lælius, feeling a hope that what you will say will be more instructive, than all those things which the Greeks have written for us." "You are creating" replied he, "much expectation from my discourse, which is a very great weight upon one, who is about to speak of matters of importance." "However great it may be," said Philus, "you will throw it off as you are accustomed to do; nor is there any danger that a dissertation from you on government will be deficient in any requisite."

XXIV. "I will do what you desire, as well as I am able," rejoined Scipio, "and will begin the discussion in conformity with the rule which I think ought to be observed in the examination of all things, if you would avoid error. That the name of the subject in discussion being agreed upon, the meaning of the name shall be defined. If this be found to be appropriate, the matter can be entered upon at once; for unless this be perfectly understood at first, we never can understand what we are disputing about. Wherefore since it is of the republic we are inquiring, let us first examine what that is we are inquiring about." Lælius having shown his acquiescence. "I do not intend, however," said Africanus, "in a matter so clear and familiar, to begin with the very origin of things; the first conjunction of the sexes; then their progeny and descendants, as some of our learned men are accustomed to do: nor shall I go into continual definitions of terms—what they are—and how many varieties of them. When I address wise men, who in war and in peace, have taken a glorious part in the affairs of a great republic, I shall not expose myself in such a manner, that the very thing under discussion shall be more intelligible, than my own explanation of it. Neither do I take upon me to pursue the subject in every direction, as a master would: nor can I promise to do it so effectually, that no omission whatever shall escape me." "It is exactly such a discourse as you promise, that I am in expectation of," said Lælius.

XXV. "A republic or commonwealth then," said Scipio, "is the wealth or common interest of the people. Every assemblage of men however, gathered together without an object, is not the people, but only an assemblage of the multitude associated by common consent, for reciprocal rights, and reciprocal usefulness. The leading cause of this congregating, is not to be ascribed so much to his weakness, as to the social principle innate with man. Our species is not a solitary and wandering one, but is so created that even when enjoying the greatest affluence * * * *

[Two pages wanting.]

XXVI. * * * * rather intuitive; for no original institution of the social state has been found, nor of the other moral virtues. These congregations therefore made for the purposes I have explained, established their first seat in some particular place for a residence. Which after being fortified by their labours and by its position, and fitted with temples and public squares, the re-union of dwellings constructed after this manner, they called a town or city. Every people therefore, formed by the assemblage of such a multitude as I have described, every city which is the settlement of a people, every commonwealth which as I have said, is the wealth of the people, must in order to be permanent, be governed by some authority. That authority however must always have a strong relation to the causes from whence the commonwealth derived its origin. It may then be delegated to one, or to some selected persons; or it may be borne by the whole multitude of the people. When therefore authority over all things, is in the control of one man, we call him king; and a commonwealth so ordered, his kingdom. When the authority is exercised by selected persons, then such a state is said to be under the government of the better class. But there is also a popular form of government, for so it is called, where all things are ruled by the people. And of any of these three modes, if the chain is in any manner kept together, which at first united men into the social pact for the sake of the common interest, I would not indeed call the mode perfect, nor say that in my opinion it was the best, but that it was to be tolerated, and that one might be preferable to another. For whether under a just and wise king, or chosen eminent citizens, or the people themselves, although this last is least to be approved of, setting aside the irregularities occasioned by the bad passions of some men, any one may see that a steady government might be preserved.

XXVII. In kingdoms however, the governed are too much deprived of common rights, and of power. Under the better class, the multitude can scarcely be partakers of liberty, as they are not admitted either to the public councils or offices: and when the government is conducted by the people, although it be justly and moderately administered, yet equality itself becomes injustice, seeing that it admits of no degrees of rank. Therefore, although Cyrus the Persian, was a most just and wise king, yet such a commonwealth, (for as I said before, it is the common property,) governed by the nod of one man, does not appear to me very desirable. And although the Massilians our clients are governed with great justice, by their chosen chief men, nevertheless in that condition of a people, there is something resembling slavery. And the Athenians at a certain period having abolished the Areopagus, conducted every thing by ordinances, and decrees of the people; yet as they had no distinctions in dignity, their state was without its ornament.

XXVIII. And this I say of these three kinds of government, not of the agitations and disturbances incidental to them, but of their tranquil and regular state. Those varieties are principally remarkable for the defects I have alluded to. Then they have other pernicious failings, for every one of these governments is travelling a dangerous road, bordering on a slippery and precipitous path. To a king so commendable, or if you choose, since I especially name him; to the amiable Cyrus; a parallel springs up in the cruel Phalaris, with all his capricious tyranny; into whose similitude the government of one man so easily slides with a downward course. To the administration of the city of the Massilians by their select chiefs, may be opposed the plot and faction of the Thirty, which took place at a certain period among the Athenians. Nor need we look farther; the very Athenian people having assumed the power over all things, and giving license to the fury of the multitude * * * * * *

Inspiration from Aristotle

[Two pages wanting.]

XXIX. * * * * * * and this great mischief arises whether under the rule of the better class, or under a tyrannical faction, or under the regal government; and even frequently under the popular form. At the same time from the various forms of government of which I have spoken, something excellent is wont to emanate. For the changes and vicissitudes in public affairs, appear to move in a circle of revolutions; which when recognized by a wise man, as soon as he beholds them impending, if he can moderate their course in the administration of affairs, and restrain them under his control; he acts truly the part of a great citizen, and almost of a divine man. Therefore I think a fourth kind of government, moderated and mixed from those three of which I first spoke, is most to be approved."

XXX. "I know" said Lælius, "that such is your opinion Africanus, for I have often heard you say so. Nevertheless, unless it is troublesome to you, I should be glad to learn which you judge best of these three kinds of government. For either it will throw some light upon * * * * * *

[Two pages wanting.]

XXXI. * * * * * * every government partakes of the nature and will of him who administers it. So that in no other state, save where the power of the people predominates, has liberty any home. Liberty the sweetest of all blessings, and which if it is not equal for all, is not liberty. For what equality can there be, I do not mean in kingdoms where slavery has no doubtful character: but in those states where all are nominally free: there indeed they give their votes, confer commands, magistracies and are solicited and intreated. But in truth they only part with that, however repugnant it may be to them, which must be conferred: things which they cannot retain, which is the reason why others seek to possess them. For they are invested with no command, have no public authority, nor are called to be judges in the tribunals: privileges which belong either to ancient families, or are purchased by money. Among a free people however, as at Rhodes or Athens, there is no citizen who * * * * *

[Two pages wanting.]

XXXII. Some assert, that when one or more in a state becomes conspicuous by his opulence or riches, disdain and pride soon break out: and the weak and indolent yield and bend under the arrogance of riches. But if the people are able to preserve their rights, they think no condition of things could be more excellent, more free, or more happy. For in their hands would be the laws, the tribunals, war, peace, treaties, and the properties and lives of all the citizens. This sort of government they think is properly called one republic, that is the common interest of the people. Wherefore it is, that the people are wont to restore commonwealths to liberty from the domination of kings, and patricians; not that kings are believed to be necessary to a free people, or that the better class are the source of power and wealth. And they deny that these advantages should not be conceded to a free people on account of the excesses of uncivilized nations: for where the people are unanimous, and every thing tends to the public safety and liberty, nothing can be more unchangeable, nothing more firm. Unanimity in such a commonwealth is very easy, where the common effort is for the public good. But from opposing interests, where one man clashes with another, discord arises. Wherefore when the senate had possession of the government, the condition of the state was never sound. In kingdoms the disadvantages are still greater; of them Ennius said

"No holy confidence or fellowship reigns there."

Wherefore as the law is the bond of civil society, and equal rights form that of the law, by what power can a community of citizens be maintained, where their condition is not an equal one? If therefore it is not expedient to equalize fortunes; if the powers of mind cannot be equalized in all, certainly then an equality of rights ought to exist, among those who are citizens of the same republic. For what is a state but a community of rights? * * * * *

[Two pages wanting.]

XXXIII. * * other governments however are deemed by them not to deserve those names, which they have chosen to arrogate to themselves. For why should I call a man who is greedy of rule, or of the sole command, and who is trampling upon an oppressed people, king, which is the title of the good Jupiter, rather than tyrant? A tyrant may be clement as well as a king may be oppressive; the matter really interesting to the people is, whether they are to serve under a gentle or a severe master: for as to being any thing but servants, that is not to be avoided. How could Lacedemon, when she was thought to excel in the science of government, possess only good and just kings, when she was obliged to take any king who was sprung from the royal blood? And the better class, who can endure them, who have arrogated to themselves in their own assemblies, a name not conceded to them by the people? For who is the man to be pronounced best, in learning, in the arts, in studies? * * * * *

[Four pages wanting.]

XXXIV. * * * * If it was done by lot, the government would be overthrown; like a ship, at whose helm, some passenger taken at hazard was placed. A nation can entrust its affairs to whom it may choose; and if it wishes to remain free, it will choose from among the best. For certainly the security of states is found in the counsels of the best citizens; especially as nature has not only ordained that they should preserve an influence over the weak by their conspicuous virtue and courage, but also that the weak should resign themselves to the government of great minds. This most desirable state of things, they say, is prevented by the erroneous opinions of men who, through ignorance of that virtue, which belongs to but few, and is seen and appreciated only by few, deem those who are sprung from a noble race, or who are opulent and wealthy, to be the best men. Under this vulgar error, when the power, not the virtues of a few, have got possession of the government; those chiefs tenaciously preserve the title of better class; a name however to which the substance is wanting. For riches, titles, and power, devoid of wisdom, of the knowledge of self-government, and that of the government of others, exhibit nothing but insolent and disgraceful pride. Nor can the condition of any city be more deplorable, than where the richest men pass for the best. But what can be more delightful than a state virtuously governed? What more illustrious than the man, who while he governs others, is himself the slave of no bad passions? Who, while he calls upon the citizens to observe the regulations he has formed, lives up to them all himself? Nor imposes any laws upon the people, which he himself obeys not, but who presents his whole life to his fellow citizens as one unbroken law. If one man could suffice to all things, there would be no need of many; and if all men could perceive what is best, and consent to it, no one would require any chiefs to be elected. The difficulty of coming to wise determinations, has transferred the rule from one king to many persons; and the error and rashness of the people, from the multitude to a few. Thus between the obstinacy of one, and the temerity of many, the better class have possessed themselves of the middle and least turbulent of all the situations: by whom if the commonwealth is well administered, the people relieved from all care and thought, must necessarily be happy: enjoying their independence through the labours of those, whose duty it is to preserve it to them; and who ought never to permit the people to think that their interests are neglected by their rulers. As to that exact equality of rights, which is held so dear by a free people; it cannot be preserved: for the people themselves, however free and unrestrained they may be, are remarkable for their deference to many persons; and exercise a great preference as it respects men and dignities. That which is called equality also, is a most unjust thing in itself: for when the same honour is enjoyed by the high and by the low, through a whole people, that very equality must be unjust; and in those states which are governed by the better class, it can never happen. These, Lælius, and some other reasons resembling them, are wont to be urged by those who chiefly praise that form of government.

XXXV. "But which, Scipio, among those three, do you chiefly approve of?" said Lælius.

Scipio. "You do well to ask, which chiefly of the three, since separately I do not approve of any of them; but should prefer to every one of them, a government constituted out of all three. But if one of them for its simplicity may be admired, I should approve of the kingly form, and give it the highest praise. For the name of king calls up at once the idea of a father, consulting with his citizens as if they were his own children; and more anxious to preserve them, than to reduce them to slavery: it being a great advantage to the weak to be sustained by the exertions and by the foresight of one pre-eminent and good man. Here however the better class profess to do the same thing to more advantage, and say there is more wisdom with numbers than with one, and at the same time equal justice and faith. But the people call out with a loud voice, that they choose neither to obey one nor many; that nothing is sweeter to the beasts of the field than liberty, which is wanting to all who serve either under the better class or under a king. Thus on the score of personal attachment, kings attract us. The better class by their wisdom; and liberty on the side of the people. So that in making the comparison, it is difficult to say which is preferable."

L. "I believe it," said he, "but if you leave this point unfinished, the other parts of the subject can scarcely be cleared up."

XXXVI. S. "Let us imitate therefore Aratus, who in his introduction to a discourse upon high matters, thought it best to begin with Jupiter."

L. "Why with Jupiter? and what has this discussion to do with the verses of Aratus?"

S. "Insomuch, that the opening of our debate may be honoured with the name of him, whom all, learned and unlearned, consent with one voice, to be the one king of all the gods and men." "What then!" said Lælius. "What do you believe in but the things which are before your eyes?" replied he. "This opinion has been established for the conduct of life, by those who have had the direction of public affairs; that the belief might prevail, that one king ruled in heaven, who with his nod, as Homer says, could tumble down Olympus; and that he should be considered as the King and Father of all. Great is the authority for it, and many the witnesses, inasmuch as all have concurred in it. Nations too have agreed, as we find in the decrees of princes, that the regal form of government was most excellent, since they imagine the gods themselves to be under the government of one king. And if we have been told that this and similar opinions have sprung from fables and the errors of the ignorant, let us listen to those who may be considered almost the common teachers of erudite men; who as it were, saw these very things with their eyes, which we scarcely are acquainted with, when we hear of them." "And who are they?" said Lælius. "They," replied he, who in their investigations of the nature of all things, have perceived a design in the universal structure of this world * * * * * *

[Four pages wanting.]

XXXVII. * * * * * * "But if you desire it Lælius, I can give you authorities in no wise barbarous, nor of too remote an antiquity."

L. I should be glad to have them.

S. You are aware that it is now somewhat less than four hundred years since this city has been governed without kings.

L. That is true; rather less.

S. What then are four hundred years, for the age of a city or state; is it such a long period?

L. It can hardly be called an adult age.

S. Then there was a king in Rome four hundred years ago?

L. And a very superb one.

S. Who before him?

L. A most just one; and from that period up to Romulus, who reigned six hundred years from the present time.

S. Then he is not so very remote.

L. Not at all. The institutions of Greece were already on the wane.

S. I submit to you now, whether Romulus was the king of a barbarous people?

L. If as the Greeks say, all men were either Greeks or Barbarians; then I am afraid he must be esteemed a king of a barbarous people. But if that epithet is appropriate to a difference of manners, rather than to languages, I think the Greeks not less barbarians than the Romans." "In relation to the matter of which we speak," said Scipio, "it is intelligence we are looking for, rather than men. If a discreet people therefore, not of a very ancient period, have preferred the government of kings, I am availing myself of testimony which cannot be deemed savage, uncivilized, or of a barbarous antiquity."

XXXVIII. "I perceive Scipio," said Lælius, "that you are sufficiently provided with testimony. But with me, as with good judges, sound argument prevails more than witnesses." "Make use of an argument then," replied Scipio, "which your knowledge of yourself can suggest to you." "What knowledge," said he.

S. Why as when by chance it happens to you to be angry with some one.

L. That occurs oftener than I could wish.

S. What! when you are in anger, do you suffer your mind to fall under the domination of that passion?

L. No, so help me Hercules. I rather imitate Archytas, the Tarentine; who on arriving at his country house, and being greatly offended at perceiving his orders had been disobeyed, "You are a miserable wretch," said he to his farmer, "and I would have you flogged to death if I were not angry." "Excellent," said Scipio. "Archytas wished to calm his anger by reflection, considering that degree of it which was not under the control of reason, to be leading on to a sort of sedition of the mind. To it add avarice, ambition, the passion for glory, and for sensual pleasures; and it will appear that there exists in the minds of men, a sort of regal controlling power, to wit, reflection. For that is the best part of the mind, and where its authority prevails, there is no room for sensuality, for anger, or for rashness.

L. So it is.

S. Do you approve therefore of a mind so disposed?

L. There is nothing I admire more.

S. Then you really do not think, reflection being driven away; that voluptuousness or the angry passions, which are without end, should have the mastery in all things.

L. Indeed I can conceive of nothing more wretched, than such a state of mind; nor of a man more debased than when under such government.

S. You prefer then all parts of the mind, to be under some government, the government of reflection?

L. I certainly prefer it.

S. Why therefore do you hesitate in your opinion about public affairs; where if the administration is transferred to many, there will be no one, as I now understand it, to take the command. And it seems that if authority is not one thing, it is nothing at all.

XXXIX. "I would ask," said Lælius, "of what consequence it is to us, whether one or many, if justice is dispensed by the latter." "Since I find Lælius," said Scipio, "that my witnesses have made no great impression on you, I shall not desist from making use of yourself as a witness to prove what I say." "Me," said he, "in what way?"

S. Why adverting to the directions you so earnestly gave to your family, when we were lately at Formianum; to obey only the orders of one person.

L. Oh! my farmer!

S. Well, at home, I suppose, several are entrusted with the management of your affairs?

L. No, only one.

S. What, your whole establishment! does no one but yourself manage it?

L. Just so.

S. Do not you therefore accede to the same conclusion in public affairs: that the government of a single person, if it is a just one, is the best?

L. I am brought to the conclusion, and must almost assent to it.

XL. You will be more inclined to that opinion, said Scipio, when omitting the analogies of one pilot, one physician, who if they are any way skilled in their arts, ought one to have the control of the ship; the other of the patient, in preference to many; I come to the consideration of greater matters.

L. What are they?

S. Are you not aware that the name of king became odious to this people, on account of the oppression and pride of one man, Tarquin?

L. Yes, I am aware.

S. Then you are aware of what haply in the course of this discussion, I may find occasion to speak. Tarquin being driven out, the people exulted with a marvellous sort of insolence of freedom. At one time driving innocent people into exile; at another, confiscating the property of many. Next came annual consuls. Then the fasces prostrated before the people—appeals in all cases. Then the mutiny of the plebeians—then a complete revolution in every thing, placing all things in the power of the people.

L. It is as you say. "It is true," said Scipio—"in peace and tranquillity, some license may be permitted when there is nothing to fear, as at sea sometimes, or in a slight fever: but like him who is at sea, when suddenly the ocean puts on its terrors, or the sick man, when his complaint oppresses him, and the assistance of one is implored: so our people in time of peace, interfere in internal affairs, threaten the magistrates, refuse submission to them, denounce them and provoke them; yet in war obey them as they would a king, preferring their safety to the indulgence of their passions. Also in our more important wars, our countrymen have constantly preferred the command to be in the hands of one, without any colleague; the extent of whose power is indicated by his name. For a dictator is so called on account of every thing being dictated by him. But in our books, Lælius, you see also that he is called master of the people."

L. It is so. "Wisely therefore did those ancients," said Scipio * * * *

[Two pages wanting.]

XLI. * * * When a people is deprived of a just king, as Ennius says, after the death of one of the best of kings,

"Long were their bosoms moved with deep regret;
Oft they together call upon his manes.

Oh, godlike Romulus! the bounteous gods
What a protector did they give in thee?
Oh father, parent, blood derived from heaven!"

Those whom the laws enjoined them to obey, they did not call lords or masters; finally, not even kings, but guardians of the country, fathers and gods. Nor without cause, for what is added,

"Thou broughtest us into the realms of light!"

They thought that life, honour, and every comfort was given to them by the justice of a king. And the same inclinations would have remained with their posterity, if the character of their kings had not changed. But you perceive that kind of government was ruined by the injustice of one man.

L. I do perceive it, and I am desirous of knowing the course of these changes, not only in our own country, but in all governments.

XLII. "It will be for you," said Scipio, "when I shall have given my opinion of that kind of government which I prefer, to give a more accurate account of the mutations in governments; although I do not think them much to be apprehended in the form I am inclined to. But a regal form of government is particularly and most certainly exposed to change. When a king begins to be unjust, that form of government perishes at once. The tyrant is, at the same time, the worst of all conditions of government, and the nearest to the best. Whom, if the better class have overturned, which for the most part happens, the commonwealth possesses 81 that second class of the three. And this is a sort of royalty; a paternal government of the principal people, for the benefit of the rest. But if the people cast out or slay the tyrant; rejoicing in their own deed, they are more moderate, as long as they know and feel the value of being so, in their endeavour to protect the commonwealth constituted by themselves. But when the populace have bent their force against a just king, and have stripped him of his kingdom; or even, as it happens very often, have tasted the blood of the better class, and have prostrated the whole republic in their madness; think not that the vexed ocean or the wildest conflagration, can be more easily kept down, than the unbridled insolence of the multitude.

XLIII. Then is produced what in Plato is so clearly described, if I can in any manner express it in Latin, a thing difficult to be done, but I will endeavour. "It is then," he says, "when the insatiable throats of the people, parched with the thirst of liberty, and led on by rash demagogues, have greedily drank, not temperate but too unalloyed draughts of freedom. Then the magistrates and chiefs, unless they are too lenient and indulgent, permitting them every excess of liberty; are pursued, impeached, insulted, and called oppressors, kings, and tyrants." I think this part of his works is known to you.

L. I am well acquainted with it.

S. Then follows, "Those who pay obedience to the magistrates, are tormented by the people, are called voluntary slaves. But those magistrates who affect to be on an equality with the lowest; and other individuals who strive to abolish all distinction between citizens and magistrates, are exalted with praises, and overwhelmed with honours. And in this condition of things, it follows, of course, that there is an unrestrained license in a government of this kind; so that every private family is without any government: and this evil extends even to the beasts. At length the father fears the son—the son disregards the father: every sort of decency is extinguished, that an open license may prevail. Nothing distinguishes the citizen from the stranger. The master pays court to his scholars, that he may be flattered by them. Teachers are despised by their disciples. Young persons take upon themselves the authority of aged ones, who abase themselves to mingle in their games, lest they become odious and burdensome to them. At last slaves give themselves all sorts of liberties. Wives assume the privileges of their husbands. Nay the dogs, the horses, the asses at length are so infected with liberty, and run kicking about so, that it is absolutely necessary to get out of their way. Wherefore from this infinite license these things result, that the minds of the citizens become so scornful and impatient, that if the least power of government is exercised, they become exasperated and will not endure it; whence they come to despise every kind of law, that they may be without the least restraint whatever."

XLIV. "You have," said Lælius, "precisely expressed Plato's sentiments."

S. Returning therefore to the subject of my discourse. "It is from this very license," he says, "which they deem to be liberty itself, that a tyrant springs up as a sapling from a root. For as the destruction of the better class arises from their overweening power, so this excess of liberty, effects the slavery of this free people. Thus all extremes of an agreeable nature, whether in the seasons, or in the fertility of the fields, or in our natural feelings, are often converted into their opposites. Especially it occurs in public affairs, where excess of liberty degenerates into public and individual slavery. Out of such licentious freedom a tyrant arises, and the most unjust and severe bondage. For by a people so untameable, or rather so outrageous, some leader is chosen out of the multitude, in opposition to the better class, now persecuted and driven from their offices: bold and dishonest, perversely persecuting those who have frequently deserved well of their country, and gratifying the people from his own means and from those of others. To whom, that he may be freed from all apprehensions on account of his private condition, authority is given and continued to him. Surrounded too by guards, as was the case with Pisistratus at Athens, at length he becomes the tyrant of the very citizens who brought him forward. Who, if he is subdued by the good, as often happens, the state is regenerated. If by the bad, then a faction is established, another kind of tyranny. The same state of things too frequently occurs in that goodly form of government of the better class, when the vices of the chiefs have caused them to deviate from their integrity. Thus do they snatch the government of the commonwealth from each other like a ball—tyrants from kings—chiefs or the people from tyrants; and factions or tyrants from them, nor does the same mode of government ever last a long time.

XLV. These things being so, the regal form of government is in my opinion much to be preferred of those three kinds. Nevertheless one which shall be well tempered and balanced out of all those three kinds of government, is better than that; yet there should be always something royal and pre-eminent in a government, at the same time that some power should be placed in the hands of the better class, and other things reserved for the judgment and will of the multitude. Now we are struck first with the great equability of such a constitution, without which a people cannot be free long; next with its stability. The three other kinds of government easily fall into the contrary extremes: as a master grows out of a king; factions from the better class; and mobs and confusion from the people. The changes too are perpetual which

power corrupts

are taking place. This cannot well happen in such a combined and moderately balanced government, unless by the great vices of the chief persons. For there is no cause for change, where every one is firmly placed in his proper station, and never gives way, whatever may fall down or be displaced.

XLVI. But I am afraid, Lælius, and you too my very discreet and respected friends, if I continue long in this strain, my discourse will appear more like that of a master or teacher to you, than as a conversation with you. Wherefore I will speak of matters known to us all, and which we have all inquired into long ago. For I am convinced, and believe, and declare, that no kind of government, either in the constitution, the planning, or the practice, is to be compared with that which our fathers have left to us, and which was adopted by our ancestors. Which if you please, since you have been desirous that I should repeat things known to yourselves, I will shew not only what it is, but that it is the best. And with our own government in view, I will if I can, have a reference to it, in whatever I may say respecting the best form of government. The which if I can follow up and effect, I shall, as I think, amply fulfil the task which Lælius has imposed on me.

XLVII. "It is your task indeed, Scipio," said Lælius, "most truly yours. For who in preference to yourself may speak of the institutions of our forefathers; you being sprung from such illustrious ancestors; or of the best form of government. The which if we now possess it, would hardly be so, if any one stood in a more conspicuous situation than yourself. Or who may venture to advise measures for posterity, when thou, having delivered the city from its greatest terrors, hast foreseen for the latest times?"

BOOK II.

I. Perceiving them all now eager to listen to him, Scipio thus began to speak. "It was old Cato, to whom as you know I was singularly attached, and whom I admired in the highest degree: to whom, either through the advice of both my parents, or from my own prepossession, I devoted myself entirely from my youth; whose conversation never could satiate me. Such was the experience of the man in public affairs, which he had for a long time successfully conducted in peace and war. His manner of speaking too, a facetiousness mixed with gravity: his constant desire also to improve himself and others; indeed his whole life in harmony with his maxims. He was wont to say, that the condition of our country was pre-eminent above all others for this cause. That among other people, individuals generally had respectively constituted the government by their laws and by their institutes, as Minos in Crete, Lycurgus in Lacedemon. At Athens, where the changes were frequent, at first Theseus, then Draco, then Solon, then Clisthenes; afterwards many others. Finally exhausted and prostrated, it had been upheld by 88 that learned man Demetrius, of Phalera. But that the constitution of our republic was not the work of one, but of many; and had not been established in the life of one man, but during several generations and ages. For he said so powerful a mind had never existed; from which nothing had escaped; nor that all minds collected into one, could foresee so much at one time, as to comprehend all things without the aid of practice and time. For which reason, as he was wont, so shall my discourse now repeat the origin of the people; for I have a pleasure in using the very words of Cato. But I shall more easily follow up my proposition in describing our own republic to you, in its infancy, its growth, in its adult, and its present firm and robust state; than if I were to create an imaginary one, as Socrates is made to do in Plato.

II. When all had approved of this, he proceeded. "What beginning, therefore, have we of the establishment of a republic so illustrious and so known to you all, as the origin of the building of this city by Romulus, born of his father Mars? For let us concede to the common opinion of men, especially as it is not only well established, but also wisely recorded by our ancestors, that those who have deserved well of us on account of our common interest, be deemed not only to have possessed a divine genius, but also a divine origin. He therefore after his birth, with Remus his brother, is said to have been ordered to be exposed on the Tiber, by the Alban king, Amulius, apprehensive lest his kingdom should be shaken. In which place, having been sustained by the teats of a wild beast, the shepherds took him, and brought him up in the labour and cultivation of the fields. It is said, that when he had grown up, he was distinguished above the rest by his corporeal strength, and the daringness of his mind. So that all who then inhabited the fields, where at this day stands the city, obeyed him willingly and without dissent. And being constituted their leader, that we may now come from fables to facts, with a strong force he took Alba-longa, a powerful and well constructed city in those times, and put the king Amulius to death.

III. Having acquired which glory, he is said first to have auspiciously thought of building a city, and of establishing a government. In regard to the situation of the city, a circumstance which is most carefully to be considered by him, who endeavours to establish a permanent government; he chose it with incredible skill. For neither did he remove to the sea, although it was a very easy thing for him with his forces, to march through the territory of the Rutulians and Aborigines; neither would he build a city at the mouth of the Tiber, to which place the king Ancus led a colony many years after. For he perceived, with an admirable foresight, that maritime situations were not proper for those cities which were founded in the hope of continuance, or with a view to empire. First, because maritime towns were not only exposed to many dangers, but to unseen ones. For the ground over which an expected enemy moves, as well as an unexpected one, announces his approach beforehand by many indications: by sound itself of a peculiarly tumultuous kind. No enemy can make a march, however forced, without our not only knowing him to be there, but even who he is, and whence he comes. But a maritime enemy and a naval force may be before you, ere any one can suspect him to be come. Nor even when he does come, does he carry before him any indication of who he is, or from whence he comes, or even what he wants. Finally by no kind of sign can it be discerned or determined whether he is a friend or an enemy.

IV. In maritime cities, too, a sort of debasing and changeable manners prevail. New languages and new customs are mingled together, and not only productions but manners are imported from abroad; so that nothing remains entire of the pristine institutions. Even they who inhabit those cities are not faithful to their homes, but with capricious inclinations and longings are carried far from them; and although their persons remain, their minds are rambling and wandering abroad. Nor did Carthage or Corinth, long before shaken, owe their ruin to any thing more than to the unsettled scattering of the citizens, who abandoned the study of agriculture and arms through their cupidity of gain and love of roaming. Many pernicious excitements too to luxury, are brought over the sea to cities by commercial importation or by conquest. Even the very amenity of the situation suggests many costly and enervating allurements. What I have said of Corinth, I know not if I may as truly say of all Greece; for almost all Peloponnessus lies on the sea, and except the Phliuntians, there are none whose lands do not extend to the coast. Beyond Peloponnessus, the Enianes, the Dorians, and the Dolopians are the only people in the interior. What shall I say of the islands of Greece? which surrounded with billows, float about as it were with the institutions and manners of their cities. These things as I said before, relate to ancient Greece; but of the colonies brought by the Greeks into Asia, Thrace, Italy, Sicily, and Africa, except Magnesia alone, which of them is not washed by the ocean? Thus a part of the Grecian shores seemed to be joined to the lands of the barbarians. For among the barbarians themselves, none were a maritime people, except the Etruscans and the Carthagenians; the one for the sake of commerce, the other for the sake of piracy. A most obvious cause of the evils and revolutions of Greece, arising from the vices of these maritime cities, which awhile ago I slightly touched upon. Nevertheless among these evils there is a great convenience. The products of every distant nation can be wafted to the city you inhabit; and in return the productions of your own lands can be sent or carried into whatever countries you choose.

V. Who then more inspiredly than Romulus could secure all the maritime conveniences, and avoid all the defects? placing the city on the banks of a perennial river, broadly flowing with an equal course to the sea. By which the city might receive what it wanted from the ocean, and return whatever was superfluous. Receiving by the same channel all things essential to the wants and the refinements of life, not only from the sea, but likewise from the interior. So that it appears to me, he had foreseen this city, at some period, would be the seat and capital of a mighty empire: for a city placed in any other part of Italy would not easily have been able to acquire such a powerful influence.

VI. As to the native defences of the city, who is so unobservant as not to have them marked and fixed in his mind? Such is the alignment and direction of the wall, which by the wisdom of Romulus, as well of succeeding kings, was bounded on every part by lofty and craggy hills: so that the only entrance, which was between the Esquiline and the Quirinal hills, was defended by a huge mound, and a very wide ditch. The citadel, surrounded by this craggy and seemingly hewn rock, had such a gallant position, that in that furious invasion of the terrible Gauls, it remained safe and intact. He choose also a place abounding in springs, and salubrious even in a pestilent region. For there are hills which while they enjoy the breezes, at the same time throw a cool shade upon the vallies.

VII. These things were done too with great celerity. For he not only founded a city, which he ordered to be called Rome, from his own name; but to establish it, and strengthen the power of the people and his kingdom, he adopted a strange and somewhat clownish plan, but worthy of a great man, whose providence extended far into futurity. When the Sabine virgins, descended from respectable families, were come to Rome to see the games, whose first anniversary he had then ordered to be celebrated in the circus, he ordered them to be seized during the sports, and gave them in marriage to the most honourable families. For which cause, when the Sabines had made war upon the Romans, and when the success of the battle was various and doubtful, he struck a league with Tatius, king of the Sabines, at the entreaty of the very matrons who had been seized: in consequence of which he admitted the Sabines into the city: and mutually having embraced each others sacred rites, he associated their king with him in the government.

VIII. After the death however of Tatius, all the power came back into his hands: although he had admitted some chiefs into the royal council with Tatius, who were called fathers, on account of the affection borne to them. He also divided the people into three tribes, named after himself, after Tatius, and after Lucumon, a companion of Romulus, who had been slain in the Sabine war: and into thirty curia, which curia he called by the names of those from among the Sabine virgins seized, at whose entreaties the peace and league had been formed. But although these things were done before the death of Tatius, yet after that event, his government became much better established, aided by the authority and counsel of the fathers.

IX. In the which he saw and judged as Lycurgus at Sparta had done, a little while before him: that states were better governed by individual command and royal power, if the authority of some of the better class were added to the energy of that kind of government. Thus sustained, and as it were propped up by the senatorial authority, he carried on many wars very successfully with his neighbours; and appropriating to himself no part of the spoil, he never ceased to enrich the citizens. At that time Romulus paid in most things attention to auspices, a custom we still retain, and greatly advantageous to the republic. For he built the city under the observance of auspices at the very beginning of the republic; and in the establishment of all public affairs, he chose an augur from each of the tribes to assist him in the auspices. He also had the common people assigned as clients to the principal men, the utility of which measure I will afterwards consider. Fines were paid in sheep and cattle: for then all property consisted in flocks, and in possessions of lands, whence the terms pecuniary and landholders were derived. He did not attempt to govern by severity or the infliction of punishments.

X. When Romulus had reigned thirty-seven years, and had established those two excellent foundations of the state, the auspices and the senate, he obtained this great meed: for when he had disappeared upon a sudden obscuration of the sun, he was deemed to have been placed among the number of the gods. A belief which no mortal had ever inspired without the greatest pre-eminence in virtue. And this is most to be admired in Romulus, that others who are said to have been deified out of the mortal state, lived in the less civilized ages of man, when the proneness to fiction was great, and the unenlightened were easily led to believe in it. But during the period of Romulus, not quite six hundred years ago, we know that learning and literature existed, and that the ancient errors peculiar to the uncultivated ages of mankind were removed. For if Rome, according to an investigation of the annals of the Greeks, was built in the second year of the seventh olympiad; the reign of Romulus occurred at that period when Greece was full of poets and musicians; and when but little faith would be given to fabulous stories, unless they were concerning very ancient things. For one hundred and eight years after Lycurgus ordained laws to be written, the first olympiad was established: which through a mistake in the name, some have thought to be founded by Lycurgus. Homer, however, by those who take the lowest period, is made to precede Lycurgus about thirty years. From which it may be gathered that Homer flourished many years before Romulus. So that there was scarce room in so intelligent an age, and amid so many learned men, for any one to establish fictions. Antiquity sometimes has received fables crudely devised, but that age already refined, and especially deriding improbable events, has rejected * * *

[About 230 letters wanting.]

* * * * Simonides was born in the fifty-sixth olympiad, by which the credit given to the immortality of Romulus may be more easily understood, seeing that the institutions of society were then so well established, organized, and known. But really so great was the force of his genius and virtue, that what men would have given no credit to for many ages in favour of any other man, was believed of Romulus upon the evidence of Proculus Julius, a countryman, who at the instigation of the fathers, in order to repel from themselves every suspicion of the death of Romulus, is said to have declared in the assembly, that he had seen Romulus on that mount which is now called Quirinal; and that he had commanded him to request

the people to erect a temple for him upon that hill; that he was a god, and was called Quirinus.

XI. "Do not you perceive therefore a new people not only sprung from the wisdom of one man, and not left crying in leading strings, but already grown up, and almost an adult?" "Indeed we perceive it," said Lælius, "and that you have entered upon a new method of discussion, which is no where to be found in the writings of the Greeks. For that pre-eminent person, whom no one has excelled in writing, has imagined to himself a situation, in which he might construct his city after his own pleasure: admirable enough perhaps, but foreign to the conduct and the manners of men. Others have discussed the subject in relation to the kinds and causes of governments, but not under any particular example of a form of government. You seem to me to be about to do both, for according to your method, you appear to prefer to attribute to others what you yourself have observed, than to imagine a state of things, as Socrates is made to do in Plato. And these matters respecting the foundation of the city, you suppose to be part of a system, which were only adopted by Romulus through necessity or chance. And your discourse is not of a desultory kind, but concerning a particular commonwealth. Wherefore proceed as you have begun, for already I perceive you are about to follow on with the other kings, as perfecting the government."

XII. "Wherefore," said Scipio, "when the senate, which Romulus had instituted out of the better class, and which had been so much favoured by the king, as to cause them to be called fathers, and their children patricians; endeavoured after the death of Romulus, to carry on the government itself without any king; the people would not endure it, and in their regret for Romulus did not cease to demand a king. Upon which the leading men prudently imagined a mode of interregnum, new and unknown to other nations. So that until a regular king was proclaimed, neither the city should be without a king, nor with one too long a period. Fearing lest from too long an enjoyment of the government, the interrex should be reluctant to lay it down, or strong enough to maintain himself in it. Even in these times, this new people perceived what had escaped the Lacedemonian Lycurgus; who esteemed it best not to choose a king, if this were indeed in the power of Lycurgus to do, but rather to be governed by any one whatever descended from the race of Hercules. But our ancestors, rude as they appear to have been, thought it behoved them rather to look to royal wisdom and virtue, than to descent.

XIII. When the great fame of Numa Pompilius had reached them, the people, leaving aside their own citizens, called in by the authority of the fathers, a king not born among them, and sent to the Curians for a Sabine to reign over Rome. When he arrived, although the people had decided that he should be king in the conventions of the curia, nevertheless he himself had a law passed in the curia concerning his own power; and as he saw the Romans through the institutions of Romulus were eager after warlike pursuits, he deemed it proper to wean them somewhat from that propensity.

XIV. And first, the lands which Romulus had acquired in war, he divided equally among the citizens; and pointed out to them, that without depopulating and pillaging, they might possess all the necessaries of life, by the cultivation of their lands. He inspired them also with the love of peace and repose, under which justice and good faith most kindly flourish; and under the protection of which, the cultivation of the fields, and the gathering of the harvest are most secure. The same Pompilius having established auspices of a superior kind, added two augurs to the ancient number, and placed five priests over sacred things from the class of the chief men. And having established those laws which we possess in our monuments, he softened, by the ceremonies of religion, minds which were inflamed by the habit and inclination of making war. He added also Flamens, Salii, and Vestal Virgins; and established with great solemnity all the branches of religion: ordaining many ceremonies to be learnt and observed, but without any expense. Thus he increased the duty of religious observances and diminished the cost of them. In like manner he established markets, games, and all the stated occasions of assembling the people together. Under which institutions, he recalled the minds of men become fierce and wild in warlike pursuits, to humanity and gentleness. When he had reigned thirty-nine years in the most perfect peace and concord, (in this we follow principally our friend Polybius, than whom no one was more accurate in ascertaining periods,) he departed from life; having strengthened every thing for the endurance of the government, by those two conspicuous virtues, religion and clemency.

XV. When Scipio had spoken these words. "Is it true, Africanus," said Manilius, "what tradition has brought down to us, that this king Numa was a disciple of Pythagoras, or is it certain he was a Pythagorean? For often we have heard this, as having been declared by old people, and understand it also to be the common opinion; yet we do not see it sufficiently proved by the authority of the public annals." "It is false," replied Scipio, "entirely so Manilius! Not false alone, but ignorantly and absurdly false; for the mendacity of those assertions is not to be endured, which we not only see are not true, but which could never have been so. It was in the fourth year of the reign of Lucius Tarquinius Superbus, that Pythagoras is ascertained to have come to Sybaris and Crotona, and those parts of Italy. For the sixty-second Olympiad announces that very arrival of Pythagoras, and the beginning of the reign of Superbus. From which it may be understood by a calculation of the reigns, that Pythagoras touched first at Italy about a hundred and forty years after the death of Numa. Nor has this fact, by those who have very diligently investigated the annals of the times, ever been thrown into any doubt." "Immortal gods," said Manilius, "how inveterate and great is the error of men! Nevertheless, I can be very well pleased in the belief, that our intelligence has not been derived from abroad, and through foreign arts, but from natural and domestic virtues."

XVI. "You will distinguish that more clearly," said Africanus, "when you perceive how the commonwealth advances and comes to the greatest perfection by a straight forward and natural course. For in this also the wisdom of our ancestors is to be praised; that many things derived from abroad, have been rendered much more perfect by us, than they were from whence they were brought, and where they first had existence. You will see also that the greatness of the Roman people has not been confirmed by chance, but by wisdom and discipline. Fortune indeed being propitious to us.

XVII. King Pompilius being dead, the people upon the proposition of an interrex, created Tullus Hostilius king, in the conventions of the curia; and he, after the example of Pompilius, consulted the people in the curia, concerning his power. His military glory was great, and important warlike affairs took place.

He constructed edifices for the senate and the *curia*, and surrounded them with military trophies. He established a law also for the declaration of war, which most justly decreed by him, he made more sacred by the solemnity of Heralds: so that every war which was not proclaimed and declared, was deemed to be impious and unjust. And observe how wisely our kings saw that some sort of deference must be paid to the people. I might say many things on that head. Tullus indeed did not venture to appear with royal insignia unless at the command of the people. For in order that it might be lawful for him to be preceded by twelve lictors with their fasces * *

[Two pages wanting.]

XVIII. * * * * * "The government which your discourse is establishing, does not creep, but rather flies towards perfection." S. "After him, Ancus Martius, grandson to Numa Pompilius by his daughter, was made king by the people, who had his elevation sanctioned by a law of the curia. Who having conquered the Latins in a war, incorporated them into the state. He also added the Aventine and Cælian Mounts to the city. The lands too which he had conquered he distributed, and made a public domain of all the forests he had taken on the sea coast. He built a city at the mouth of the Tiber, and planted a colony there. When he had thus reigned twenty-three years, he died. "This king also is to be praised," said Lælius, "but the Roman history is obscure: for although we know who was the mother of this king, we do not know who was his father." S. "So it is" said he, "but generally the names of the kings only of those times are conspicuous."

XIX. "But it is here that we first perceive the city to have become more intelligent by extrinsic information. For not a gentle stream flowed from Greece into this city, but an abundant flood of arts and knowledge. It is stated that one Demaratus, a Corinthian, a principal man, and of much honour and authority in his own city, and of an easy fortune, not being able to endure Cypselus, the tyrant of the Corinthians, fled with a great deal of money, and betook himself to a flourishing city of Etruria, among the Tarquinians. When he had heard that the domination of Cypselus was confirmed, being an independent and powerful man, he renounced his country, and was received a citizen by the Tarquinians: and in that city he fixed his home and establishment. Where when he had begotten two sons from one of the Tarquinian matrons, he instructed them in all the arts after the manner of the Greeks * * * *

[Two pages wanting.]

XX. * * * * * He was well received in the city, and became intimate with king Ancus on account of his learning and liberal knowledge. So much so that he shared all his counsels, and might be deemed even a partner in his kingdom. For there was a great affability in him, and an extreme readiness in aiding, protecting, and doing liberal acts to every citizen. Martius therefore being dead, L. Tarquinius was created king by the united suffrages of the people; for thus he had changed his name from his Grecian one, that in every thing he might be seen to imitate the manners of the people. Having caused his accession to be confirmed by a law, he doubled the pristine number of the fathers; calling those whose opinions he first asked, ancient fathers of the greater families; and those whom he had admitted, he called the lesser families. Then he established the knights; after the manner that has obtained unto our day. He could not change the names of the Titienses, of the Rhamnensians, or the Luceres, when he wished to do so; because Attus Nævius being then Augur in great reputation, would not consent to it. We see the Corinthians chose formerly to assign cavalry for the public service, and to have their expenses defrayed by taxes on orphans and widows. But to the old troops of horse he added others, and made twelve hundred knights. He doubled this number after he had subdued the Equi in war, a powerful and ferocious race, which threatened the affairs of the Roman people. And when he had driven the Sabines from the walls of the city, he scattered them with his horse and conquered them. It is he whom we understand to have instituted the great games, which we call Roman, and to have made a vow during the Sabine war, while in battle, that he would raise a temple on the capitol to the great and good Jupiter. He died when he had reigned thirty-eight years.

XXI. "Now," said Lælius, "is that saying of Cato very certain, that the constitution of the state is not the work of one moment or one man: for it is evident how great an accession of good and useful institutions occurred under each reign. But he comes next, who appears to me to have looked farther than them all into the nature of government." "So it is," said Scipio, "for after him Servius Sulpicius is stated first to have reigned without the command of the people. He is said to have been born of a Tarquinian slave: she having conceived him by some client of the king. Brought up among the number of the servants, when he attended at the royal table, he did not suppress those sparks of genius, which even then shone forth in the boy: so shrewd was he in every thing, whether in business or conversation. Wherefore Tarquin, who at that time had only young children, became so attached to Servius, that he was generally thought to be his son; and with great pains instructed him in all those arts, which he himself had been taught, after the very superior manner of the Greeks. But when Tarquin had perished by the plots of the sons of Ancus, Servius, as I before said, began to reign, not by the command, but by the assent and sufferance of the people. For when Tarquin was falsely said to be alive, and sick from the effects of his wound; he declared the law in royal pomp, and discharged debtors with his own money. Conducting himself with much courtesy, he declared that he pronounced the law at the command of Tarquin. He did not commit himself to the fathers, but Tarquin being buried, he conferred with the people about himself, and being authorised to reign, he had his accession confirmed by a law of the curia. And first he avenged himself by war, for injuries received from the Etruscans, * * * * * *

[Two pages wanting.]

XXII. * * he inscribed eighteen centuries of horse in the great register. Afterwards having set apart a great number of equestrians from the mass of the whole people, he distributed the rest of the citizens into five classes, and divided the old from the young: and classed them in such a manner, that the suffrages were not in the power of the multitude, but of the landed proprietors. He was careful of what ought always to be observed in government; that numbers alone should not have the ascendency. Which classification if it were unknown to you, should be explained by

RIP Cicero, u would have loved timelines + being able to print pictures

me. You will perceive the plan was such, that the centuries of horse with six suffrages, (a century being added from the carpenters on account of their great utility to the city,) and the first class, make eighty-nine centuries: to which from the one hundred and four centuries, for so many remain; if only eight are added, the whole power of the people is obtained: and the much greater multitude comprehended in the ninety-six centuries remaining, is neither excluded from voting, lest it should seem disdainful; nor is it made too effective, lest it should be dangerous. In the which matter he was very circumspect even as to terms and names. Those from among the wealthy he called "assiduos" from paying their taxes in money. Those who possessed no more than one thousand five hundred pieces of brass, or those who were polled in the register without any possessions whatever, he called proletaries; as if progeny only; that is, as if nothing but population might be expected from them. But of those ninety six centuries, more were enumerated in one century, than almost in the whole first class. Thus the right of suffrage was not prohibited to any one by law, and that class had a greater weight of suffrage, which had most at stake in the preservation of good government. As to public criers, men hired for parade, clarion players, horn players, and proletaries, * * * *

[Four pages wanting.]

XXIII. * * * * * Was sixty-five years more ancient, being built thirty-nine years before the first olympiad. And the very ancient Lycurgus had the same thing in view. This equality therefore, and this triple nature of public affairs appears to me to have been common to us and to those people. But what is peculiar in our republic, and than which nothing can be more admirable, I will look very critically into if I am able; as nothing similar is to be found in any government. For these things which I have adverted to, were so mingled in this state, and among the Lacedemonians, and the Carthagenians, that they were not properly balanced. For in whatever government any one man enjoys perpetual power, especially royalty, although even a Senate may exist in it, as was the case at Rome under the kings, and in the laws of Lycurgus at Sparta; and even granting the people some share in the government, as was the fact under our kings: still that royal name will stand pre-eminent, nor can a government of that kind be any thing but a kingdom, or be called otherwise. But such a form of government is especially subject to change for this reason; that it easily falls into the most unprofitable courses, precipitated thereunto by the vices of one man. For the royal form of government itself, not only is not to be condemned, but I know not whether it is not greatly to be preferred to the other simple forms, if I could approve of any simple form of government. But only as long as it preserves its proper character, which is that the safety, the equality, and tranquillity of the citizens, are to be preserved by the justice, the wisdom, and the perpetual power of one man. Many things however are altogether wanting to a people subject to a king. Liberty among the first: which is not that we may live under a just master, but under none at all. * * *

[Two pages wanting.]

XXIV. For some time fortune prosperously accompanied this unjust and cruel master in the administration of affairs. He subdued all Latium in war, and took Suessa, an opulent and well stored Pometian city. Enriched with great spoils of gold and silver, he accomplished the vow of his ancestor in the building of the capitol. He established colonies, and according to the institutions of those from whom he had derived his origin, he sent magnificent gifts, as offerings of his spoils, to Apollo at Delphos.

XXV. Here the very circle is set in motion, whose natural movement and revolution you learn to distinguish from the beginning. For the very head of discretion in civil matters, upon which all our discourse turns, is to observe the ways and bendings of public affairs; so that when you perceive what way any thing inclines, you may either keep it back, or meet it by opposing other things to it. For the king of whom I speak, having stained himself first with the murder of a good king, no longer preserved his integrity of mind, and wished to inspire fear himself, because he dreaded every sort of punishment for his wickedness. Afterwards borne up with his victories and riches, he exulted with insolence, and imposed no restraint on his own conduct, or the licentiousness of his followers. Wherefore when his eldest son had used violence with Lucretia, the wife of Collatinus, and daughter of Tricipitinus, and the noble and chaste woman had inflicted death upon herself on account of that injury; L. Brutus, a man pre-eminent in mind and courage, released his fellow citizens from that unjust yoke of a cruel slavery: who, although he was a private citizen, sustained the whole government, and was the first who taught in this city, that no man was to be considered insignificant, when the public liberties were to be preserved. Under which leader and head, the whole city being in commotion, as well with the recent complaints of the family and kindred of Lucretia, as with the remembrance of the many wrongs done by the haughtiness of Tarquin himself, and his sons; the banishment of the king, his children, and his whole race was pronounced.

XXVI. Do not you perceive then how a master may spring out of a king, and how a form of government from being good, may become the very worst, through the vice of one man. This is that master over the people, whom the Greeks call tyrant; him only they esteem a king, who consults like a parent with the people, and preserves those over whom he is placed, in the most prosperous condition of life. A sort of government very good as I have said, but bordering upon and inclining to a very pernicious one. For when this king deviates into unjust rule, at once he becomes a tyrant, and an animal more hideous, more destructive, and more odious, in the eyes of gods and men cannot be conceived: surpassing, although in the human form, the most monstrous wild beasts in cruelty. How can he be rightly called a man, who observes no fellowship of humanity with his fellow citizens, no communion of law with the whole race of man? But a more proper place to speak of this will occur, when circumstances will suggest to us to speak of those, who have sought to usurp the Government over free cities.

XXVII. You have here then the origin of a tyrant, for the Greeks would have this to be the name of an unjust king. Our ancestors indeed have called all who have had an exclusive and perpetual dominion over the people, kings. Thus Spurius Cassius, M. Manilius, and Spurius Mælius, are said to have wished to establish a kingdom, and even * * * * * *

[Two pages wanting.]

XXVIII. Lycurgus gave the name of ancients at Lacedemon, to that too small number of twenty-eight, to whom he wished the whole authority of counsel to be confided, while the sole command should be held by the king. Wherefore our ancestors translating and adopting that term, those whom he called ancients, they called a senate: as we have already stated Romulus to have done with the select fathers. Nevertheless, the royal title, and its strength and power were always pre-eminent. Impart too something of power to the people, as was done by Lycurgus and Romulus, and you will not satisfy them with freedom, but you will inflame them with the passion of liberty, when you have only permitted them to taste of power. The fear indeed will always hang over them, lest they should have an unjust king, which generally happens. The fortune therefore of a people is, as I said before, very uncertain, which is placed in the will or conduct of one man.

XXIX. Wherefore this first form, example, and origin of a tyrant, is found by us in that very government which Romulus instituted with auspices, and not in that, which Plato says Socrates imagined to himself in that peripatetic discourse. And as Tarquin subverted the whole fabric of royalty, not because he grasped a new sort of authority, but because he made a bad use of it; so let us oppose to him another; a good man, wise and expert in every thing useful and dignified in civil life: a tutor and steward as it were of the commonwealth, for so may be called whoever is the ruler and governor of a state. Imagine to yourselves that you recognise such a man; one who can protect the state, both by his counsel and conduct. And since the name of such a man has not been alluded to in this discourse, and that a character of this kind will be frequently treated of in what remains to be said * * * * * *

[Twelve pages wanting.]

XXX. * * * * * * Plato described a state more to be desired, than to be hoped for upon the smallest scale. He did not constitute things as they might exist, but in such a manner as the nature of civil affairs might be considered. As to myself, if in any way I am able to accomplish it, with the same principles which he had in view, I will look, not into the picture and shadow of a state, but into a most powerful republic; that I may appear to touch, as it were, the true cause of every public good and evil. After these two hundred and forty years of regal government, and indeed a little more, including the interregnums, Tarquin being banished, the royal title was as odious to the Roman people, as it had been regretted after the death, or rather the disappearance of Romulus, and as much as they wanted a king then, in like manner, after the expulsion of Tarquin, they could not endure the name of one.

XXXI. Under this feeling our ancestors then expelled Collatinus, who was innocent, through apprehension of his family connexions, and the other Tarquins from disgust at their names. From the same cause too P. Valerius ordered the fasces to be lowered when he began to speak before the people; and had his building materials taken to the foot of the Velia, as soon as he perceived the suspicions of the people to be raised on account of his having begun to build in a more conspicuous part of the Velia, the very place where King Tullus had dwelt. He also, in the which he greatly deserved the name of Publicola, had that law passed for the people, which was first carried in the meetings of the centuries, that no unfriendly magistrate should put to death, or flog any Roman citizen for appealing. The pontifical books however declare appeals to have existed under the kings; the augural records show it also. The twelve tables too in many laws indicate that it was lawful to appeal from every judgment and punishment. What is brought down to us by tradition, of the Decemvirs who wrote the laws, being created without any appeal, sufficiently shows that the other magistrates had not the power of judging without appeal. The law, too, which for the sake of concord passed in the consulate of Lucius Valerius Potitus, and M. Horatius Barbatus, men very justly popular; sanctioned the principle, that no magistrate should be created without appeal. Nor did the Portian laws, which are three as you know of the three Portii, contain any thing new except the confirmation of it. Publicola therefore, upon the law in favour of appeal being published, immediately ordered the axes to be taken from off the fasces, and the next day had Sp. Lucretius appointed to him as his colleague: being his superior in age, he ordered his own lictors to go to him; and first established the custom that lictors should precede each of the consuls, alternate months, lest the ensigns of command among a free people, should be as numerous as in a kingdom. There was something more than mediocrity in this man, as I consider him: who having given a moderate liberty to the people, preserved more easily the authority of the chiefs. Nor do I repeat these things, now so old and obsolete to you, without cause. I select examples of men and things drawn from illustrious persons and times, to which the remainder of my discourse shall be applied.

XXXII. In such a manner the senate governed the commonwealth in those days, that though the people were free, still they interfered in but few things. Public affairs were principally managed under the authority, and by the rules and customs of the senate. And although the consuls possessed their power only for a year, it was royal in its nature and effect. And this was strenuously preserved, as necessary to the preservation of the influence of the nobles and principal chiefs, that nothing should be established in the meetings of the people, which was not sanctioned by the authority of the fathers. In these very times too, T. Larcius was appointed dictator, about ten years after the first consuls. A new kind of authority, very much resembling, as we perceive, the royal power. But all great matters were conducted by the authority of the principal men, the people submitting to it. And great events took place in those times in war, under renowned men in the supreme command, from among those very dictators and consuls.

XXXIII. But what belongs to the very nature of things, as that a people emancipated from kings, should take a little more power to themselves; was brought about not long after, about the sixteenth year, in the consulate of Postumus Cominus, and Sp. Cassius. Not in the right way perhaps, but it is of the nature of public affairs frequently to deviate from what is right. For observe what I said in the beginning, that unless an equable compensation prevails in a state, in the laws, in offices, in emoluments; so that the magistrates enjoy their proper degree of power; the chief men their authority in council, and the people their liberties, such a state of the government cannot remain unchanged. For when the city was in commotion on account of the pressure of their debts, the people first occupied the Sacred Mount, then the Aventine. Nor could the discipline even of Lycurgus keep the Greeks 114 within those restraints. In the reign of Theopompus, at Sparta, those five whom they call Ephori; the ten too in Crete, who are called Cosmoi; arose against the royal power, as the tribunes of the people did against the consular authority.

XXXIV. Perhaps there was a mode by which our ancestors might have relieved the pressure of the law of debt, which had not escaped Solon, the Athenian, some short time before, and which our senate adopted not long after, when on account of the infamous conduct of a creditor, the citizens were liberated from the general oppression, and voluntary bondage on account of debt abolished in future. And always at such periods, when the common people are exhausted by contributions in times of public calamity, some relief and remedy is to be devised for the common safety. Which the senate having neglected to do, sufficient cause was given to the people to create two tribunes during a sedition of the plebeians, with intent to weaken the power and authority of the senate; which nevertheless remained a grave and great body, bringing forward in the service of the state the wisest and bravest men, and strengthening it by arms and counsel. And their authority was the greater, because far excelling all others in honour, they were less conspicuous for voluptuousness, and not much signalized by their wealth. Their high worth also was the more esteemed in the state, because in private life they diligently assisted individuals by their advice, and by substantial services.

XXXV. In which situation of the republic, the quæstor accused Sp. Cassius, who enjoyed the highest degree of favour with the people, and was contriving a usurpation of the government; and as you have heard, when his own father stated himself to be satisfied of his guilt, the people assenting to it, he put him to death. It was a grateful thing also to the people, when Sp. Tarpeius, and A. Aternius, consuls, about fifty-four years after the first consuls, carried a law in the meetings of the centuries concerning fines. Twenty years afterwards when L. Papirius, and P. Pinarius, censors, by pronouncing fines, converted the strength of the flocks of many private individuals to the public use; a light valuation of cattle was ordained in the law on fines, during the consulate of C. Julius and P. Papirius.

XXXVI. But some years before, when the senate enjoyed the greatest authority, the people being very patient and obedient, a new plan was instituted. The consuls and the tribunes of the people abdicated the magistracy, and ten men were created with the greatest authority, and without appeal, who were to possess the supreme power, and to inscribe the laws. Who when they with great equity and prudence, had written ten tables of laws, appointed ten other decemvirs for the following year, whose faith and justice are not in like manner praised. From which college, however, comes that praiseworthy act of C. Julius, who stated that in his presence a body had been dug out of the chamber of a patrician, L. Sestius. Although he had supreme power, and as decemvir was without appeal, he admitted him to bail, refusing to lose sight of that most excellent law, which forbids sentence to be pronounced on the head of a Roman citizen, unless in the meetings of the centuries.

XXXVII. A third decemviral year followed under the same men, they being unwilling to appoint others. In this condition of the commonwealth, which I have often already stated not to be lasting, because it is not equable to all the orders of the state, the chief men had the whole government in their hands; the most noble decemvirs being always preferred. No tribunes of plebeians opposed to them, no other magistrates associated with them, and no appeal left to the people against death and stripes. Wherefore on account of the injustice of these men, a great disturbance suddenly arose, and a revolution took place in the whole commonwealth. They added two tables of iniquitous laws, in which the very marriages which were even permitted to strangers, were forbidden by an inhuman law, lest the plebeians should connect themselves with the fathers; which law was afterwards abrogated by the plebicist Canuleius. In all things they conducted themselves libidinously, cruelly, and avariciously towards the people. Upon that celebrated and well known affair contained in many literary records, in which one Decimus Virginius on account of the outrage of one of the decemvirs, slew his virgin daughter with his own hand in the Forum, and fled lamenting to the army which was then on Mount Algide; the soldiers abandoned the war they were then engaged in, and as was before done for a similar cause, first came to the sacred mount, and next to the Aventine * * * * *

[Eight pages wanting.]

XXXVIII. When Scipio had spoken these things, and all by their silence were expecting the remainder.—"Since my seniors here, Africanus," said Tubero, "ask you no questions, hear from me what I still find wanting in your discourse." "Most cheerfully," replied Scipio. "You appear to me," said he "to have been pronouncing the eulogium of our republic, when Lælius was inquiring not respecting ours, but of government in general. Nor have I learnt from your discourse, by what discipline, or by what customs or laws, a republic like the one you praise, can be constituted or preserved."

XXXIX. "I think," said Africanus, "we shall by and by have a more appropriate occasion, Tubero, of discussing the establishment and preservation of states. In respect to the best kind of government, I deem myself to have sufficiently answered the inquiries which Lælius made. First I pointed out three kinds of government that might be endured, and to these three their very pernicious opposites: that no one among them was the best, but that one moderately balanced from all three, was preferable to either of them. That I have availed myself of our state for an example, was not with a view to define the best form of government, for that could be done without an example. But in truth, that a great state might present the very picture, such as reason and language might describe it to be. But if without going to the example of any people, you are desirous of finding that perfect condition of government, then look at the image which nature presents to us * * *

[A great number of pages wanting here.]

XL. S. * * * a character I have been looking for, and have been desirous of arriving at.

L. The discreet statesman, perhaps?

S. The very same.

L. You have all those present who are so numerous: or you can begin with yourself. "I wish," said Scipio, "it was proportionally so in the whole senate. However, he is a discreet man, who as we have frequently seen in Africa, seated on a monstrous wild and ferocious animal, governs and directs him; making him kneel down, not with blows, but with a slight sign."

L. I know, and have often seen it when I was Lieutenant to you.

S. So the Indian or Carthagenian governs a wild beast, and renders it docile and gentle with humane conduct. But that intellectual principle which is hidden in the souls of men, and which is called a part of the soul, does not bridle or tame one easily subdued, whenever it accomplishes it, which rarely happens. For that ferocious animal must be restrained * * * *

[Either four or eight pages are wanting here.]

XLII. "Already," said Lælius, "I see the man I expected, so greatly endowed, and charged with such duties." "With this duty only," replied Africanus, "for in this one almost all the rest are included. That in his thoughts and actions he never deviate from himself, so that he may call upon others to imitate him, and that he may offer himself in the purity of his mind and his life, as a mirror to his fellow citizens. For as in stringed instruments or pipes, as well as in singing with voices, a certain harmony is to be formed with distinct sounds, an interruption to which cannot be borne by refined ears; this kindred and harmonious concert being produced by the modification of dissimilar voices. So a government temperately organized from the upper, the lower and middle orders blended together, harmonizes like music by the agreement of dissimilar sounds. And that which in song is called by musicians, harmony, is concord in a state; the strongest and best bond of safety in every republic; yet which without justice cannot be preserved.

[Many pages wanting.]

XLIV. "I assent entirely to it," said Scipio, "and declare freely to you, that we must esteem in nothing all that we have said upon government, or that may remain farther to be said, unless it be established, not only that it is false, that injustice is necessary, but that this is most true; that without the most perfect justice, no government can prosper in any manner. But if you please, thus far for to day. The remainder, for many things remain yet to be said, we will defer until to-morrow." When this was approved, an end was put to the discussion for that day.

BOOK III.

[Four or eight pages wanting.]

II. * * * * The intelligent principle having found man endowed with the faculty of uttering rude and imperfect sounds, enabled him to separate and distinguish them into articulations. Thus words were affixed to things as signs of them, and man, once solitary, became united to man, by the sweet bond of conversation. By the same intelligence, the inflexions of the voice, which we find to be infinite in number, are all distinguished and expressed, by the invention of a few marks, which enable us to hold a correspondence with the absent, to indicate our inclinations, and to preserve a record of things past. To this the knowledge of numbers was added, a thing not only necessary to life, but at once immutable and eternal. Which first led us to consider the heavens, to look upon the motion of the planets with interest, and the numbering of the nights and days * * * *

[Eight or ten pages wanting.]

III. * * * * Whose minds rose to a loftier pitch as I before said, that they might execute or discover something worthy of the gift they had received from the gods. Wherefore let those who have treated upon the moral conduct of life, be deemed by us, great men, as they are; learned men; masters of truth and virtue. Yet let it be admitted that civil rights, and the government of a people, whether they are the fruits of men experienced in the management of public affairs, or, as the fact has been, the result of their literary leisure, be least despised; causing as they do to spring up in great minds, as we have often seen, an incredible and divine virtue. For if any one to those faculties which the mind has from nature, and to those talents which civil institutions produce, hath added also the learning, and the more various knowledge of things, in which men engaged in the discussion of those books are versed, there is no one who ought not to prefer such a man to all others. For what can be more excellent, than when the practice and habit of great affairs is joined to a perfect knowledge of the theory of the science of them? Or what more perfect can be imagined than P. Scipio, C. Lælius, and L. Philus; who that they might omit nothing appertaining to the high character of enlightened men, to the knowledge of our domestic and ancient customs, united the learning received from Socrates? Wherefore he who determined and effected both, that is, instructed himself as well in the institutions, as in the philosophy of the ancients, I think has accomplished every thing with praise. But if a choice must be made between those two paths to excellence, and if to any one, that tranquil way of life passed in the best studies and sciences may appear happier, still certainly an active, civil life is more illustrious and more laudable. The greatest men derive their glory from such a life, as M. Curius * * * *

Whom none could overcome with arms or gold.

[Six pages wanting.]

IV. * * * Nevertheless this difference existed in their two different modes: the one unfolded the principles of nature by their studies and by their eloquence; the others by their institutions and by their laws. This commonwealth alone has produced many, if not altogether to be deemed sages, since that title is so cautiously bestowed, yet worthy of the greatest praise; for they cultivated the precepts and discoveries of sages. Wherefore civil governments are to be extolled and ever will be, since in the nature of things, to constitute a commonwealth which shall be lasting, is one of the greatest efforts of mind: and thus if we only enumerate one for every country, what a multitude of excellent men do we find. For if we permit our minds to take a survey of that famous Greece, of Italy, Latium, or the Sabine and Volscian people; the Samnites, the Etrurians; next the Assyrians, the Persians, the Carthagenians. If these * * *

[Twelve pages wanting.]

V. * * * "Truly," said Philus, "you have imposed a fine task upon me, wishing me to undertake the justification of what is wrong." "Surely," said Lælius, "you are afraid lest in using the same arguments which are wont to be brought forward against justice, you may appear to hold such opinions yourself; you who are almost the only example left of ancient probity and faith. But your habit of discussing both sides of the question, in order more easily to get at the truth, is very well known." "Well, well," said Philus, "I will do as you wish, and defile myself with my eyes open: for since those who search for gold do not refuse to do it; we who are looking for what is right, a thing much more precious than gold, assuredly ought not to avoid any thing that is disagreeable. And I wish, since I am about to make use of another man's opinions, it was possible for me to make use of his tongue also. Now, however, L. Furius Philus, must say what Carneades, a Greek in the habit of saying whatever he pleased * * *

[Four pages wanting.]

VIII. * * * But the other has filled four pretty large books with the subject of justice. From Chrysippus I have never looked for any thing very great or magnificent; since he reasons in a particular way of his own, and examines things rather by the force of words, than the weight of facts. It was for those distinguished men, to raise up that prostrate virtue, and elevate it to the divine heights of wisdom. A virtue which stands alone as it were, greatly munificent and liberal; which loves every thing better than itself, and is born more for others, than for its own interests. Nor was the inclination wanting to them: for what other cause had they for writing, or what motive soever? In genius they excelled all. But the cause was greater even than their inclination and strength. The right indeed concerning which we inquire, is something civil, not natural; if it were, justice and injustice would be the same things to all men, as hot and cold, bitter and sweet things are.

IX. Now however, if any one borne upon the chariot with winged serpents, of which Pacuvius speaks, could survey with his eyes, and look down upon the many and various nations and cities; he might see chiefly among that unchanging race of the Egyptians, which preserves in its records the memory of so many events and ages, an ox esteemed as a god, which the Egyptians call Apis; and many other strange things among them, among which wild beasts consecrated into the number of the gods. Then in Greece, where as with us, magnificent temples are consecrated containing human images, which the Persians considered impious. For which cause alone, Xerxes is said to have ordered the temples of the Athenians to be burnt; considering it to be wicked to shut the gods up within walls, whose residence was the whole universe. Afterwards Philip who had it in contemplation, and Alexander who carried it into effect, gave as reasons for making war against the Persians, that they avenged the temples of Greece; which the Greeks did not think of repairing, that the devastation might be an eternal monument to posterity of the infamy of the Persians. How many, as the Taurians in Axinum, as Busiris the king of Egypt, as the Gauls, the Carthagenians, have thought it a grateful and pious duty to the gods, to immolate men. But the institutions of life differ so much, that the Cretans and Etolians esteem it honourable to steal: the Lacedemonians used to say that all lands were theirs which they could reach with a shaft. The Athenians were wont to swear even publicly, that every soil was theirs, which produced oil and corn. The Gauls consider it shameful to produce grain by labour, and therefore go armed to harvest other people's lands. But we, the most just of men, to make our own olive and vineyards more valuable, do not permit the transalpine nations to plant them: in doing which we are said to act prudently; it is not called acting justly. By which you may understand there is a wide distance between prudence and equity. Lycurgus, the founder of the best laws, and the most equal rights, gave the lands of the wealthy to be cultivated by the lower class in the state of servitude.

X. But if I were to describe the various kinds of laws, of institutions, of customs and manners, not only so different among such divers nations, but even in a single city, or in this, I could demonstrate them to have been changed a thousand times. Our friend Manilius here, an interpreter of laws, will tell you that other laws exist now concerning the legacies and inheritances of women, than those he was wont to speak of in his youth, before the Voconian law was passed; which very law, indeed proposed for the advantage of the men, is full of injustice towards the women. For why should a woman not have possessions? Why should a vestal appoint an heir, and her mother not? Why if limits were to be put to the possessions of women, should the daughter of Crassus, if she were an only daughter, possess thousands legally, when mine could not possess two or three hundred * * * * * *

[Two pages wanting.]

XI. * * * * * * If these rights were thus sanctioned in us, all men would have the same rights, and would not have different rights at different periods. But if it is the duty of a just and good man to obey the laws, I would ask which are they to be? Or shall he obey all indiscriminately? But virtue does not admit of uncertainty, nor nature endure inconstancy. The strength of law consists in punishment, not in our natural justice. Natural right therefore does not exist. Whence it follows, that men are not made just by nature. But it is said, although there are various laws, still good men, by natural inclination, pursue what is just in itself, and not what is assumed to be so; because it is the part of a good and just man, to render that justice to every one which he is deserving of. Now, first, are we in any wise just to the dumb beasts? For men, not of mediocrity, but great and learned; Pythagoras and Empedocles, declare that all animals possess the same degree of right, and denounce unatoning punishments to hang over those by whom any animal is outraged. It is wicked therefore to injure the brutes. * * * * * *

[Eight pages wanting.]

XII. * * * * * * what we call wisdom, urges us to increase our wealth, our riches, and to extend our possessions. How could that great commander who formerly carried the limits of his empire into Asia; how could he govern, bear sway, reign, have dominion, and the full enjoyment of voluptuousness, unless he took something from others? But justice orders us to spare all, to consult the welfare of mankind, to give to every one his own, and to abstain from every thing that is sacred, every thing that is public, every thing which is not our own. What therefore is to be done? If wisdom is consulted, riches, power, wealth, honours, authority, empire, are open to individuals and nations. But since it is the public interest we are discussing, instances of a public nature will illustrate better; and as the same degree of right is in both, I shall advert to the wisdom of a nation, and I shall omit the rest. Our own nation, which Africanus in his discourse yesterday, traced to its origin, whose empire already extends over the earth, has it, once least of them all, become so by justice or wisdom? * * * * * *

[Four or eight pages wanting.]

XIV. For all who possess the power of life and death over a people are tyrants, yet they prefer to be called kings by the name of the good Jupiter. When certain persons through the influence of their riches, their class, or other circumstances, possess themselves of the government, it is a faction. Yet they call themselves, the better class. If the people however are uppermost and rule every thing at their own pleasure, that is called liberty; nevertheless it is licentiousness. But when one fears another, man mistrusting man, and one class another, then because no one confides, a sort of pact is made between the people and the great, from whence that combined form of government springs, which Scipio has praised. So that neither nature, or the will is the mother of justice, but weakness. For when one thing is to be chosen out of three, either to do injustice without permitting it to be done to you; or to do it and permit it also; or neither one or the other: the best is to do it with impunity if you can; the second best is neither to do it, nor suffer it to be done to you: the worst of all is to be eternally fighting now on account of your own aggressions, now on account of those of others * * * * *

[An unknown number of pages wanting.]

* * * Except the Arcadians and the Athenians, who, I suppose, fearing lest at some period this decree of justice might appear, have feigned themselves to be sprung from the earth, like the little mice we see in the fields.

XVI. To these things, others are wont to be added principally by those, distinguished for their honesty in discussion, and having more weight for that reason. Who when engaged in the inquiry of what constitutes a good man, frank and plain as we wish to find him, are not themselves crafty, hardened, and malicious in argument. They deny that the wise man is good only because goodness and justice are pleasing to him from their nature; but because the lives of good men are free from apprehension, care, solicitude and danger. Whereas bad men have always a sting goading their souls, and judgment and punishment are always present to their eyes. That there is no emolument, no advantage arising from injustice, so great as to compensate the fear, and the constant thought that some punishment is impending * * * * *

[Four or eight pages wanting.]

XVII. I ask if there be two men, one of them of the very best kind; equitable, perfectly just, of exemplary faith: the other singular for his wickedness and audacity: and suppose the community in such an error, that the good man passes for a wicked and dishonest one; while the bad one has the reputation of perfect probity and good faith. And through this general delusion of the citizens, the good man is harassed, arrested, bound, his eyes put out, condemned, thrown in chains, tortured in the fire, banished. Wanting every thing, at last he appears to all to be deservedly the most wretched of men. On the other hand, the bad man is praised, sought after, caressed by all. Honours of every kind, authority, power, and every advantage conferred upon him from all sides. A man, finally, in the estimation of all deemed the very best, and worthy of the highest gifts of fortune. Who would be so insane as to hesitate which of these two he would choose to be?

XVIII. As it is with individuals, so it is with nations. No community is so stupid, as not to prefer commanding by injustice, to serving according to justice. I shall not go far back for examples. Being consul, you assisting me in council; I had to examine the Numantine treaty. Who is ignorant that Pompey made that treaty, and that Mancinus was concerned in the same affair? This last most excellent man supported the proposition I carried from the consultation in the senate; the other most earnestly opposed it. Those who valued modesty, integrity, and good faith preferred

Mancinus: yet for his reasoning, counsel, and policy, Pompey took the lead of him * * * *

[An unknown number of pages wanting.]

XXIX. * * * * * Ti. Gracchus was vigilant for the interests of the people, but neglected the rights of the Latins and the treaties with the allies. If such customs and license should spread themselves wider, and our empire be changed from right to force, so that those who until now voluntarily obey us, should 134 be ruled only by terror; although it has been vigilantly preserved for us, who are of the present age; yet I should be very solicitous about our posterity, and about the immortality of the republic, which might be perpetual, if the institutions and manners of our forefathers were preserved.

XXX. When Lælius had thus spoken, all present expressed themselves to have been very much delighted by him, but Scipio, among the rest, as if quite elated with pleasure, "many causes," said he, "indeed Lælius, hast thou often defended, in such a manner that I can by no means compare our colleague Servius Galba to thee; whom when he lived thou preferredest to all; nor in truth any of the attic orators * * *

[Twelve pages wanting.]

XXXI. * * * * * Therefore that common interest, that is the commonwealth, who can recognize it when all are oppressed by the cruelty of one; when no bond of Law exists, nor that consent of congregated society, which constitutes a people. And this very condition of the Syracusans: a celebrated city, as Timæus says, the first among the Greeks, and the most beautiful of them all: its harbour embosomed within the walls, its canals running through the city: its broad streets, its porticoes, temples, fortifications, all these did not help to constitute a commonwealth, while Dionysius reigned. The people had no part in them, for the very people belonged to one man. Therefore where there is a tyrant, it is not a vitiated commonwealth, as I said yesterday, but reason compels us to declare plainly that no commonwealth at all exists.

XXXII. "Indeed" said Lælius, "you speak very clearly, and I already perceive the drift of your discourse.

S. You see therefore, that when every thing is in the power of a faction, neither can that be properly called a commonwealth.

L. I judge it plainly so.

S. And most rightly do you judge, for what was the condition of the Athenians, when after that great Pelopponesian war, thirty men were most unjustly placed in the command of that city? Did the ancient glory of the city, the admirable nature of its buildings, its theatre, gymnasia, its noble porticoes, its citadel, or the admirable works of Phidias, or the magnificent port of Piræus, did they constitute a commonwealth? "Not in the least" said Lælius, "because indeed the common interest was not thought of."

S. How was it at Rome, when the Decemvirs existed without appeal, in that third year, when liberty itself had parted with its privileges?

L. Nothing was left to the people, and truly it was necessary to bring them to that point, that they might recover their rights.

XXXIII. S. I come now to the third kind, that in which some inconsistency will perhaps be perceived, where all things are said to be done by the people, and to be in the power of the people. When the multitude orders punishments to be inflicted in any manner that it pleases, ordering, seizing, keeping, dissipating every thing whatever they choose, can you then Lælius, deny that to be a republic, where all things belong to the people, and when indeed we define a republic to be a commonwealth?" "There is nothing," said Lælius, "I would sooner deny to be a republic, than where all things are in the power of the multitude. We did not consider that they had a republic among the Syracusans, or at Agrigentum, or at Athens when they were under tyrants, or at Rome when under the decemvirs. Nor do I see how the name of republic is appropriate when the multitude rules. Because first, as you have happily defined it to me, Scipio, a people does not exist, but where it is held together by consent of law; and this sort of mob, is as much a tyrant as if it were one man. Indeed it is more mischievous, for nothing is more ferocious than the wild beast which assumes the name and form of the people. Nor is it right, when the property of maniacs is placed by law under the guardianship of kindred, that * * *

[Eight pages wanting.]

XXXIV. * * * of it, it may with as much propriety be said that it is a republic and a commonwealth, as it may be said of a kingdom. "And much more," said Mummius, "for a king being one, is more like a master; but where many good men are at the head of affairs in a republic, nothing can be more happily constituted. But I certainly prefer a kingdom to the sway of a democracy; which third and most vicious kind of government remains for you to explain."

XXXV. To this Scipio replied, "I recognize well Spurius, your steady aversion to the popular mode, and although it might be treated with less aversion than you are wont to do, nevertheless I agree, that of all these three kinds, no one is less to be approved of. I do not however agree with you that the better class are to be preferred to a king; for if it is wisdom which governs a state, of what consequence is it, whether it resides in one, or in many? But in our discussion we are led into a sort of error. When we call them the better class, nothing can be conceived more excellent, for what can be imagined more desirable than the best? When however a king is mentioned, an unjust king occurs to our minds. We do not nevertheless intend to speak of an unjust king, in our examination of this royal kind of government. Think of Romulus, Pompilius, and Tullus as kings, and perhaps you will not be so displeased with that kind of government.

M. What sort of praise then is left for a democratic government?

S. What did you think, Spurius, of the Rhodians, with whom we were together; did you see nothing like a commonwealth there?

M. Indeed I did, and least of all to be blamed.

S. You say well. But if you remember all were alike; sometimes plebeians, sometimes senators; and by turns discharging during certain months their functions as senators; the other months they remained in the ranks of the people. In both capacities however they had the privilege of being present at the meetings for deliberation, and equally in the theatres and in the courts, great matters and all others were judged; so numerous was the multitude and so great its power that * * * * *

BOOK IV.

II. * * * * * * How conveniently the orders are set down; the ages, the classes. The equestrian order where the senate votes. Too many foolishly seek to abolish that useful institution, hoping that through some Plebecists procuring the sale of the horses, they may get a largess.

III. Look now at the other provisions so wisely made, that the citizens may enjoy a happy and honest state of society, for that is the very motive for their union; and which government ought to secure to men, by institutions and laws. In the first place, as to puerile discipline for free-born young men, respecting which the Greeks have laboured so much in vain; and the only matter about which our guest Polybius reproaches the negligence of our institutions. No defined system, or of a public nature, or uniform for all, was decreed by the laws.

[Four or eight pages wanting.]

IV. * * * * * * nor naked when at an age of puberty. So deep did they seek as it were to lay the foundations of modesty. But how absurd the exercises of youth in the Grecian Gymnasia; how trifling that drilling of young boys: what loose and unrestrained manners permitted to them. I say nothing of the Eleans and Thebans, among whom free license and permission was given to the young people to indulge in sensuality. The Lacedemonians too, when they allowed every sensual indulgence short of violence, among their youth, were destroying what they were granting such a slight protection to. "I clearly understand, Scipio," said Lælius, "that in these practices of the Greeks, which you reprehend, you had rather attack the most illustrious people, than your favourite Plato, whom you do not assail at all, especially * * * * *

BOOK V.

II. * * * * * * No prerogative more royal than the administration of justice, in which was comprehended the expounding of rights, for individuals were accustomed to seek justice from kings. On which account the lands, the fields, the groves, the extensive and rich grazing districts were defined, which belonged to the sovereign, and were all managed without any care or labour on his part; that none of the cares of private business, might abstract him from the affairs of the public. Nor was any man an umpire or arbitrator of any legal contention, but all things were decided by royal judgments. And it seems to me, that our Numa chiefly adopted this ancient custom from the kings of Greece. For the others, although they also discharged this function, yet a great many of them waged wars, and occupied themselves in establishing the rules of war. But that long peace of Numa, was the parent of law and religion to this city. He also was the writer of those laws which you know to be extant: all which is appropriate to the very citizen whose character we are drawing * * * * * *

[An unknown number of pages wanting.]

III. S. Do you think there is any harm in his being acquainted with the nature of roots and seeds?

M. None, if only his work is not neglected.

S. But do you think it to be properly the study of a farmer?

M. Not in the least; for the cultivation of the land would often be unattended to.

S. Therefore, as a farmer is acquainted with the nature of his soil, a steward with the nature of letters, and each can turn from the amusement of theory to the greater utility of practice; so this our ruler may be thoroughly conversant with the knowledge of rights and of laws; he may have looked even into the very fountains of them: but let not his consultations, his constant readings, and his writings occupy him too much; but let him be as it were both steward and farmer to the commonwealth. Let him be skilled in the principles of law without which no man can be just; let him not be ignorant of civil law: but let it be as the pilot who studies the stars; the physician who studies the nature of plants and minerals; each turning his knowledge to the benefit of his art, without permitting it to impede the practical use of his vocation * * *

[An unknown number of pages wanting.]

IV. * * * * In those states where the good look for praise and honour, and fly from ignominy and disgrace. Not so much restrained by apprehension of the penalties established by law, but by a sentiment of self-respect, which nature has planted in man, a sort of dread of deserved censure. This sentiment the ruler of a state strengthens by public opinion, and confirms by education, and by institutions, that shame may deter the citizen from crime as much as fear. But these considerations properly belong to renown, and shall be more abundantly considered.

V. Life, however, and the comfortable enjoyment of it, are constituted by legal marriages, lawful children; the keeping hallowed the seats of the penate gods, and the domestic lares; that all may enjoy public and private comforts. Without good government, private life cannot be agreeable, nor can any one be more happy than in a well regulated state * * * *

ON THE LAWS

§ 1.1 BOOK I

ATTICUS: This is the very grove, and this the oak of Arpinum, whose description in your poem on Marius, I have often read. If, my Marcus, that oak is still in being, this must certainly be it, but it appears extremely old.

QUINTUS CICERO: Yes, my Atticus, my brother's oak tree still exists, and will ever flourish, for it is a nurseling of genius. No plant can owe such longevity to the care of the agriculturist as this derives from the verse of the poet.

§ 1.2 ATTICUS: How can that happen, my Quintus? How can poets bestow immortality on trees? It seems to me that in eulogizing your brother, you flatter your own vanity. QUINTUS: You may rally me as much as you please, but as long as the Latin language is spoken, this oak of Marius will not lose its reputation; and as Scaevola said of my brother's poem on Marius, it will "Extend its hoary age, through countless years." Do not your Athenians maintain that the olive near their citadel is immortal, and that tall and slender palm tree which Homer's Ulysses says he beheld at Delos, do they not make an exhibition of it to this very day? and so with regard to other things, in many places, whose memorial endures beyond the term of their natural life. Therefore this acorn-bearing oak, on which once lighted

Jove's golden Eagle, dazzling as the sun, still flourishes before us. And when the storms of centuries shall have wasted it, there will still be found a relic on this sacred spot, which shall be called the Oak of Marius.

§ 1.3 ATTICUS: I don't doubt it, my Quintus; but there is one question I would ask, not of you, but of the poet Marcus himself, whether the tree is indebted for its celebrity to his verses alone, or whether the circumstance they record really happened in the history of Marius?

MARCUS CICERO: I will answer you frankly, my Atticus. But you must first inform me what you think of the tradition which asserts, that not far from your house at Rome, Proculus Julius beheld our first king Romulus walking after his decease, and that he heard him declare his desire of being invoked as a God, of being entitled Quirinus, and of having a temple there dedicated to his memory? Tell me also what you think of the tradition of the Athenians, who maintain that not far from your Athenian villa, Boreas made a stolen match with Orithyia, for so runs the story.

§ 1.4 ATTICUS: For what purpose do you ask me such questions as these?

MARCUS: For no purpose at all, unless it be to convince you that we had better not enquire too critically into those remarkable accounts which are thus handed down by tradition.

ATTICUS: But this ingenious apology will not deter some from enquiring whether many of the statements in your Marius are true or false; and some will expect the greater accuracy from you, since Arpinum was your own birth place as well as that of Marius, and the events of his life must be fresh in your memory.

MARCUS: I have certainly no ambition to gain the reputation of a liar. But some of these inquisitors, my Atticus, are really too severe. It is preposterous to expect an exact statement of matters of fact in a poem of this nature, as if I had written it not as a poet, but as an eye witness upon oath. I doubt not the same critics would make the same objections if I were to versify on Numa's intercourse with Egeria, and the Eagle which dropped a coronet in the head of the first Tarquin.

QUINTUS: I understand you, my brother; you think that the historian must maintain a closer adherence to fact than the poet.

MARCUS: Certainly. History has its laws, and poetry its privileges. The main object of the former is truth in all its relations: the main object of the latter is delight and pleasure of every description. Yet even in Herodotus, the father of Greek history, and in Theopompus, we find fables scarcely less numerous than those which appear in the works of the poets.

ATTICUS: Stop there; I have found the occasion I wanted, and I shall not hesitate to urge my suit.

MARCUS: What suit, Atticus?

ATTICUS: We asked you, long ago, or rather implored you, to write a History of the Roman empire, for we conceive if you undertook this literary enterprise, even in the historical department, we should yield no palms or laurels to Greece. And if you will listen to my opinion, it seems to me that you owe this gift, not only to the affection of those who are delighted with your writings, but you likewise owe it to your country, that since you have saved her constitution, you should endeavour to adorn her annals, A good history of our country is a desideratum in our national literature, as I know by my own experience, and as I have often heard you declare. Now there is no man more likely than yourself to give general satisfaction in a work of this kind, since by your own avowal, it is of all the forms of composition that which most demands the eloquence of the orator. You would therefore be doing us a great favour if you would undertake this work, and devote your time to a complete history of Rome, which is unknown to most of our fellow-citizens, or at least neglected by them. For after the annals of the chief Pontiffs, which are very contracted, if we come to the book of Fabius, or Cato, whom you are always eulogizing, or the treatises of Piso, Fannius, and Venonius, though one of them may excel another, are they not all extremely defective? The contemporary of Fannius, Coelius Antipater, adopted a bolder style of expression. His energy was indeed somewhat rude and rough, without polish or point, but he did what he could to recommend a manly and truthful eloquence. But unfortunately he had for his successors a Claudius, an Asellio, who, far from improving on him, relapsed into the former dullness and insipidity.

I scarcely need to mention Attius. His loquacity is not without its fine points, though he has derived them not so much from the great Grecian authors, as from the Latin scribblers. His style is full of littlenesses and atrocious conceits. His friend Sisenna, far surpasses all our historical writers whose compositions have yet been published, for of the rest we cannot judge. He has, however, never gained a name among the orators of your rank; and in his history he betrays a sort of puerility. He seems to have read no

Greek author but Clitarchus, and him he imitates without reserve, but even when he succeeds in his imitation, he is still far enough from the best style. Therefore the task of historian of right belongs to you, and we shall expect you to accomplish it, unless Quintus can bring forward any reasonable objections.

QUINTUS: I have nothing to say against it. Indeed we have often talked over the subject together, and I have made the same request as yourself; but we could never quite agree in our views of the subject.

ATTICUS: How so?

QUINTUS: Why we differed respecting the epoch from whence such a history should commence its narrative. In my opinion, it ought to begin with the origin of our state and nation, for the accounts that have hitherto been published respecting our primitive antiquities are so written as never to be read. My brother, on the other hand, wishes to confine himself to the events that have happened in our own times, so as only to describe those public affairs in which he himself bore a part.

ATTICUS: In this respect I rather agree with him. For the grandest events in Roman history are probably those that have taken place within our own recollection. He would then be able to illustrate the praises of our noble friend Pompey, and describe the memorable year of his own consulship. These memoirs, I imagine, would be far more interesting than any thing he could tell us respecting Romulus and Remus.

MARCUS: I know, my Atticus, that you and other friends have long urged me to this undertaking, nor should I be at all unwilling to attempt it, if I could find more free and leisure time. But it is vain to enter on so extensive a work while my mind is harassed with cares, and my hands are full of business. Such literary enterprises demand a perfect freedom from anxieties and political embarassments.

§ 1.9 ATTICUS: How then did you find leisure and vacation enough to compose more books than any of our Roman authors?

MARCUS: Why certain spare times (subcisiva tempora) occur to every man, and these I was unwilling to lose. For instance, if I spent a few days in rusticating at my country seat, I employed them in composing a part of the essays I had determined to write. But for an historical work, it is impossible to do it justice unless one can procure a regular vacation for a considerable period. My mind is thrown into a miserable state of suspense, when after fairly commencing a literary task, I am obliged to defer its conclusion to a future occasion; nor can I so easily recover the train of ideas in works so interrupted, as bring my essays to their appropriate conclusion, without rest or intermission.

ATTICUS: You therefore require a prolonged vacation for the historical treatise we propose, and a full allowance of holidays, with all their freedom and tranquility.

MARCUS: I conceive myself the better entitled to such vacations as I advance in life, since I am desirous, after the method of our ancestors, to continue the custom of giving magisterial advice to my clients, and thus to discharge the offices of old age gracefully and honourably. In such a situation, I should be able to compose not only the historical work you require, but others, still more extensive and diversified, with all desirable accuracy.

ATTICUS: I fear that few will accept such an apology for your retirement, and that you will be obliged to speak in public as long as you live. I regret this the more, as the lapse of years will compel you to change your manner of delivery, and your style of eloquence. Thus, your friend Roscius the actor, in his old age, was forced to give up his most brilliant modulations, and to adapt the instrumental accompaniments to a slower measure. Thus you also, my Cicero, will find it necessary daily to relax from those lofty conflicts of oratory to which you have been accustomed, till your eloquence gradually assimilates to the bland garulity of the philosophers. Since, however, the extremest old age is still capable of executing some duties of patriotism, I see that your retirement will not hinder you from advising your clients.

QUINTUS: I think that the citizens of Rome would readily grant you this kind of secession from public affairs, if you still consented to advise in legal matters. It is at your own option to try the experiment whenever you please.

MARCUS: Your advice, my Quintus, would be excellent if there were no danger in taking such a step. But I fear in thus seeking to diminish my labours I should rather increase them. I have an objection to thus aggravating the toil of public causes and prosecutions (which I never attempt to plead without full and mature study) by the addition of this professional interpretation of the laws, which would not distress me so much by its wearisomeness as by its tendency to deprive me of that preparation for speaking, without which I never dared to enter on any considerable pleadings.

ATTICUS: Whichever course, you resolve on, my Cicero, we have some spare time as you call it, at present, and I should be very glad if you would employ it in enlightening us respecting the laws of the state. On this subject I am sure you can give us something better than has hitherto been published. For even from your earliest youth, I remember, you have studied the laws, when I went like yourself to hear the lectures of Scaevola, nor did I ever find you so addicted to oratorical pursuits as to neglect your legal ones.

MARCUS: You seek to engage me in a long discussion, my Atticus. However, I will not hesitate to undertake it unless Quintus prefers some other subject. If not, I will frankly tell you all I know about it, since at present we seem to be at leisure.

QUINTUS: I shall listen to you with the greatest pleasure, for what better subject can be discussed, or how can the day be spent more profitably?

MARCUS: Let us go then to our accustomed promenade, where they have placed the benches on which we may recline after we have had sufficient exercise. I flatter myself that our discussion will be agreeable enough, since we shall be able each of us to throw light on the several topics with which we are personally most familiar..

ATTICUS: Let us go then, and enter on our investigations, as we walk along the bank of the river under the shadow of its foliage. And to begin with the beginning, let me ask I pray you, what is your opinion respecting the nature of Law?

MARCUS: What is my opinion?—I hardly dare to deliver it, lest it should appear presumptuous. For we have had many great men in Rome, who have made it their profession to expound it to the people, and explain its doctrines and practice. But though they professed to be acquainted with its majestic theory, they were rather familiar with its minuter technicalities. What can be grander or nobler than jurisprudence? or what can be more insignificant and quibbling than the practice of lawyers?—necessary as it is for the people. Not that I think that those who adopt this profession are altogether ignorant of the principles of universal legislation; but they are far more attentive to the civil law, which gives them a hold on the interests of the people. Are then the sublime and recondite principles of jurisprudence less necessary or less useful? Certainly not. It is these you wish me to elucidate and illustrate, and not the formal regulations of our civic economy. You ask me not to write treatises on the rights (stillicidiorum ac parietum) of common sewers and partition walls; and to compose forms of stipulations and judgments. These have been already most diligently prepared by clerks in office, and are decidedly lower than the topics which, I suppose, you expect me to discuss.

§ 1.15 ATTICUS: For my part, if you ask my opinion, I should reply, that after having given us a treatise on the Commonwealth, you cannot consistently refuse us one on the Laws. In doing so, you will imitate the example of your favorite Plato, the philosopher whom you chiefly admire and love with an especial affection.

MARCUS: Do you wish then, that we should emulate that conversation which Plato held with Clinias of Crete, and Megillus of Lacedaemon, which he describes as taking place one summer day under the cypress trees of Cnossus, and in its sylvan avenues: where, after discoursing and arguing respecting the best kind of commonwealths and their appropriate laws, he sauntered with his delightful friends?—Do you wish that thus we also, walking beneath these lofty poplars, along these green and umbrageous banks, and sometimes reposing, should investigate the same subjects somewhat more profoundly than is usual among barristers?

§ 1.16 ATTICUS: I am delighted with your proposal.

MARCUS: But what says my brother Quintus?

QUINTUS: I can imagine nothing more agreeable.

MARCUS: I admire your choice. For in no kind of discussion can we more advantageously investigate the facilities which man owes to nature, and the capacity of the human mind for the noblest enterprises. We will discuss the true objects of thought and action, for which we were born and sent into the world, and the beautiful association and fellowship which bind men together by reciprocal charities: when we have fathomed these grand and universal principles of morals, we shall discover the true fountain of laws and rights.

§ 1.17 ATTICUS: In your opinion, then, it is not in the edict of the praetors, as the majority of our modern lawyers pretend, nor in the rules of the Twelve Tables of our Statutes, as the ancient Romans maintained, but in the sublimest doctrines of philosophy, we must seek the true source and obligation of jurisprudence.

MARCUS: It is for this reason, my Atticus, that you do not ask me to explain to you the formalities of legal practice, and the technical replications and rejoinders of our professional pleadings. These, indeed, deserve much study and respect, inasmuch as they have occupied the attention of many great men, and are at present expounded by a most eminent lawyer (Servius Sulpicius Rufus) with admirable ability and skill.

But the subject of our present discussion soars far higher, and comprehends the universal principles of equity and law. In such a discussion therefore on the great moral law of nature, the practice of the civil law can occupy but an insignificant and subordinate station. For according to our idea, we shall have to explain the true nature of moral justice, which is congenial and correspondent with the true nature of man. We shall have to examine those principles of legislation by which all political states should be governed. And last of all, shall we have to speak of those laws and customs which are framed for the use and convenience of particular peoples, which regulate the civic and municipal affairs of the citizens, and which are known by the title of civil laws.

QUINTUS: You take a noble view of the subject, my brother, and go to the fountain-head of moral truth, in order to throw light on the whole science of jurisprudence: while those who confine their legal studies to the civil law too often grow less familiar with the arts of justice than with those of litigation.

MARCUS: Your observation, my Quintus, is not quite correct. It is not so much the science of law that produces litigation, as the ignorance of it, (potius ignoratio juris litigiosa est quam scientia). But more of this bye-and-bye.

With respect to the true principle of justice, many learned men have maintained that it springs from Law. I hardly know if their opinion be not correct, at least, according to their own definition; for Law (say they) is the highest reason, implanted in nature, which prescribes those things which ought to be done, and forbids the contrary. This, they think, is apparent from the converse of the proposition; because this same reason, when it is confirmed and established in men's minds, is the law of all their actions. They therefore conceive that the voice of conscience is a law, that moral prudence is a law, whose operation is to urge us to good actions, and restrain us from evil ones. They think, too, that the Greek name for law (νόμος), which is derived from νέμω, to distribute, implies the very nature of the thing, that is, to give every man his due. For my part, I imagine that the moral essence of law is better expressed by its Latin name, (lex), which conveys the idea of selection or discrimination. According to the Greeks, therefore, the name of law implies an equitable distribution of goods: according to the Romans, an equitable discrimation between good and evil.

The true definition of law should, however, include both these characteristics. And this being granted as an almost self-evident proposition, the origin of justice is to be sought in the divine law of eternal and immutable morality. This indeed is the true energy of nature, the very soul and essence of wisdom, the test of virtue and vice. But since every discussion must relate to some subject, whose terms are of frequent occurrence in the popular language of the citizens, we shall be sometimes obliged to use the same terms as the vulgar, and to conform to that common idiom which signifies by the word law, all the arbitrary regulations which are found in our statute books, either commanding or forbidding certain actions.

ATTICUS: Let us begin, then, to establish the principles of justice on that eternal and universal law, whose origin precedes the immeasurable course of ages, before legislative enactments were in being, or political governments constituted.

§ 1.20 QUINTUS: By thus ascending to first principles, the order of our discourse will be more methodical, so as to conduct us by agreeable gradations to the practical bearings of the subject.

MARCUS: You wish, then, that we should seek for justice in its native source, which being discovered, we shall afterwards be able to speak with more authority and precision respecting our civil laws, that come home to the affairs of our citizens?

QUINTUS: Such is the course I would advise.

ATTICUS: I also subscribe to your brother's opinion.

MARCUS: Well then, I shall endeavour to describe a system of Laws adapted to that Commonwealth, which Scipio declares to be most desirable in those Six Books which I have written under that title. All our laws, therefore, are to be accomodated to that mixed kind of political government there recommended. We shall also treat of the general principles of morals and manners, which appear most appropriate to such a constitution of society, but without descending to particular details.

QUINTUS: You therefore derive the principles of justice from the principles of nature, to investigate which is the main object of all our discussions.

ATTICUS: Certainly, and when she is our guide, we are not very likely to err.

§ 1.21 MARCUS: Grant me, then, my Atticus, (for I know my brother's opinion already),—grant me that the entire universe is overruled by the power of God, that by his nature, reason, energy, mind, divinity, or some other word of clearer signification, all things are governed and directed; for if you will not grant me this, I must proceed to prove it.

ATTICUS: Respecting the existence of God, and the superintendence of divine providence, I grant you all you can desire. But owing to this singing of birds and babbling of waters, I fear my friends can scarcely hear me.

MARCUS: You are quite right to be on your guard, my Atticus; for even the best men occasionally fall into a passion, and what would your fellow-students, the Epicureans, say, if they heard you denying the first article of that notable book, entitled the Chief Doctrines of Epicurus, in which he says that "God takes care of nothing, neither of himself nor of any other being?"

§ 1.22 ATTICUS: Pray proceed, for I am waiting to know what advantage you mean to take of the concession I have made you.

MARCUS: I will not detain you long. Since you grant me the existence of God, and the superintendence of Providence, I maintain that he has been especially beneficent to man. This human animal—prescient, sagacious, complex, acute, full of memory, reason and counsel, which we call man,—is generated by the supreme God in a more transcendent condition than most of his fellow-creatures. For he is the only creature among the earthly races of animated beings endued with superior reason and thought, in which the rest are deficient. And what is there, I do not say in man alone, but in all heaven and earth, more divine than reason, which, when it becomes ripe and perfect, is justly termed wisdom?

§ 1.23 There exists, therefore, since nothing is better than reason, and since this is the common property of God and man, a certain aboriginal rational intercourse between divine and human natures. This reason, which is common to both, therefore, can be none other than right reason; and since this right reason is what we call Law, God and men are said by Law to be consociated. Between whom, since there is a communion of law, there must be also a communication of Justice.

Law and Justice being thus the common rule of immortals and mortals, it follows that they are both the fellow-citizens of one city and commonwealth. And if they are obedient to the same rule, the same authority and denomination, they may with still closer propriety be termed fellow-citizens, since one celestial regency, one divine mind, one omnipotent Deity then regulates all their thoughts and actions.

This universe, therefore, forms one immeasurable Commonwealth and city, common alike to gods and mortals. And as in earthly states, certain particular laws, which we shall hereafter describe, govern the particular relationships of kindred tribes; so in the nature of things doth an universal law, far more magnificent and resplendent, regulate the affairs of that universal city where gods and men compose one vast association.

When we thus reason on universal nature, we are accustomed to reason after this method. We believe that in the long course of ages and the uninterrupted succession of celestial revolutions, the seed of the human race was sown on our planet, and being scattered over the earth, was animated by the divine gift of souls. Thus men retained from their terrestrial origin, their perishable and mortal bodies, while their immortal spirits were ingenerated by Deity.

From which consideration we are bold to say that we possess a certain consanguinity and kindred fellowship with the celestials. And so far as we know, among all the varieties of animals, man alone retains the idea of the Divinity. And among men there is no nation so savage and ferocious as to deny the necessity of worshipping God, however ignorant it may be respecting the nature of his attributes.

§ 1.25 From whence we conclude that every man must recognize a Deity, who considers the origin of his nature and the progress of his life.

Now the law of virtue is the same in God and man, and cannot possibly be diverse. This virtue is nothing else than a nature perfect in itself, and developed in all its excellence. There exists therefore a similitude between God and man; nor can any knowledge be more appropriate and sterling than what relates to this divine similitude.

Nature, attentive to our wants, offers us her treasures with the most graceful profusion. And it is easy to perceive that the benefits which flow from her are true and veritable gifts, which Providence has provided on purpose for human enjoyment, and not the fortuitous productions of her exuberant fecundity. Her liberality appears, not only in the fruits and vegetables which gush from the bosom of the earth, but likewise in cattle and the beasts of the field. It is clear that some of these are intended for the advantage of mankind, a part for propagation, and a part for food. Innumerable arts have likewise been discovered by the teaching of nature; for her doth reason imitate, and skilfully discover all things necessary to the happiness of life.

With respect to man this same bountiful nature hath not merely allotted him a subtle and active spirit, but moreover favoured him with physical senses, like so many guardians and messengers. Thus has she improved our understanding in relation to many obscure principles, and laid the foundation of practical knowledge; and in all respects moulded our corporeal faculties to the service of our intellectual genius. For while she has debased the forms of other animals, who live to eat rather than eat to live, she has bestowed on man an erect stature, and an open countenance, and thus prompted him to the contemplation of heaven, the ancient home of his kindred immortals. So exquisitely, too, hath she fashioned the features of the human face, as to make them symbolic of the most recondite thoughts and sentiments.

§ 1.27 As for our two eloquent eyes (oculi nimis arguti), do they not speak forth every impulse and passion of our souls? And that which we call expression in which we infinitely excel all the inferior animals, how marvellously it delineates all our speculations and feelings! Of this the Greeks well knew the meaning, though they had no word for it.

I will not enlarge on the wonderful faculties and qualities of the rest of the body, the modulation of the voice, and the power of oratory, which is perhaps the greatest instrument of our influence over human society. These matters do not belong to the occasion of our present discourse, and I think that Scipio has already sufficiently explained them in those books of mine which you have read.

As the Deity, therefore, was pleased to create man as the chief and president of all terrestrial creatures, so it is evident, without further argument, that human nature has made the greatest advances by its intrinsic energy; that nature, which without any other instruction than her own, has developed the first rude principles of the understanding, and strengthened and perfected reason to all the appliances of science and art.

ATTICUS: Good heavens, my Cicero! from what a tremendous distance are you deducing the principles of justice! However, I wont hurry too eagerly to what I expect you to say on the Civil Law. But I will listen patiently, even if you spend the whole day in this kind of discourse, for assuredly these are grander topics which you introduce as a preamble than those to which they prepare the way.

MARCUS: You may well describe these topics as grand, which we are now briefly discussing. For of all the questions on which our philosophers argue, there is none which it is more important thoroughly to understand than this, that man is born for justice, and that law and equity are not a mere establishment of opinion, but an institution of nature. This truth will become still more apparent if we investigate the nature of human association and society.

There is no one thing more like to another, more homogeneous and analogous, than man is to man. And if the corruption of customs, and the variation of opinions, had not induced an imbecility of minds, and turned them aside from the course of nature, no one would more nearly resemble himself than all men would resemble all men. Therefore whatever definition we give of man, it must include the whole human race. And this is a good argument, that no portion of mankind can be heterogeneous or dissimilar from the rest; because, if this were the case, one definition could not include all men.

In fact, reason, which alone gives us so many advantages over beasts, by means of which we conjecture, argue, refute, discourse, and accomplish and conclude our designs, is assuredly common to all men; for the faculty of acquiring knowledge is similar in all human minds, though the knowledge itself may be endlessly diversified. By the same senses we all perceive the same objects, and that which strikes the sensibilities of the few, cannot be indifferent to those of the many. Those first rude elements of intelligence which, as I before observed, are the earliest developments of thought, are similarly exhibited by all men; and that faculty of speech which is the soul's interpreter, agrees in the ideas it conveys, though it may differ in the syllables that express them. And therefore there exists not a man in any nation, who, adopting his true nature for his true guide, may not improve in virtue.

Nor is this resemblance which all men bear to each other remarkable in those things only which accord to right reason. For it is scarcely less conspicuous in those corrupt practices by which right reason is most cruelly violated. For all men alike are captivated by voluptuousness, which is in reality no better than disgraceful vice, though it may seem to bear some natural relations to goodness; for by its delicious delicacy and luxury it insinuates error into the mind, and leads us to cultivate it as something salutary, forgetful of its poisonous qualities.

An error, scarcely less universal, induces us to shun death, as if it were annihilation; and to cling to life, because it keeps us in our present stage of existence, which is perhaps rather a misfortune than a desideratum. Thus, likewise, we erroneously consider pain as one of the greatest evils, not only on account of its present asperity, but also because it seems the precursor of mortality. Another common delusion obtains, which induces all mankind to associate renown with honesty, as if we are necessarily happy when we are renowned, and miserable when we happen to be inglorious. In short, our minds are all similarly susceptible of inquietudes, joys, desires and fears; and if opinions are not the same in all men, it does not follow, for example, that the people of Egypt who deify dogs and cats, do not labour under superstition in the same way as other nations, though they may differ from them in the forms of its manifestation.

But in nothing is the uniformity of human nature more conspicuous than in its respect for virtue. What nation is there, in which kindness, benignity, gratitude, and mindfulness of benefits are not recommended? What nation in which arrogance, malice, cruelty, and unthankfulness, are not reprobated and detested! This uniformity of opinions, invincibly demonstrates that mankind was intended to compose one fraternal association. And to affect this, the faculty of reason must be improved till it instructs us in all the arts of well-living. If what I have said meets your approbation, I will proceed; or if any of my argument appears defective, I will endeavour to explain it.

ATTICUS: We see nothing to object to, if I may reply for both of us.

MARCUS: It follows, then, in the line of our argument, that nature made us just that we might participate our goods with each other, and supply each others' wants. You observe in this discussion whenever I speak of nature, I mean nature in its genuine purity, and not in the corrupt state which is displayed by the depravity of evil custom, which is so great, that the natural and innate flame of virtue is often almost extinguished and stifled by the antagonist vices, which are accumulated around it. But if our true nature would assert her rights, and teach men the noble lesson of the poet, who says, "I am a man, therefore no human interest can be indifferent to me,"—then would justice be administered equally by all and to all. For nature hath not merely given us reason, but right reason, and consequently that law, which is nothing else than right reason enjoining what is good, and forbidding what is evil.

Now if nature hath given us law, she hath also given us justice,— for as she has bestowed reason on all, she has equally bestowed the sense of justice on all. And therefore did Socrates deservedly execrate the man who first drew a distinction between the law of nature and the law of morals, for he justly conceived that this error is the source of most human vices.

It is to this essential union between the naturally honorable, and the politically expedient, that this sentence of Pythagoras refers:— "Love is universal: let its benefits be universal likewise."

§ 1.34 From whence it appears that when a wise man is attached to a good man by that friendship whose rights are so extensive, that phenomenon takes place which is altogether incredible to worldlings, and yet it is a necessary consequence, that he loves himself not more dearly than he loves his friend. For how can a difference of interests arise where all interests are similar? If there could be such a difference of interests, however minute, it would be no longer a true friendship, which vanishes immediately when, for the sake of our own benefit, we would sacrifice that of our friend.

I have made these preliminary remarks, to prepare you the better for the main subject of our discourse, in order that you may more easily understand the principle, that nature herself is the foundation of justice. When I have explained this a little more at large, I shall come to the consideration of that civil law to which all my arguments refer.

QUINTUS: Then you have not much to add, my brother, for the arguments you have already used have sufficiently proved to Atticus and myself that nature is the fountain of justice.

ATTICUS: How could I maintain any other opinion, since you have proved to us, first, that the gods have been pleased to enrich and adorn us with their gifts, on purpose that we might administer them justly. Secondly, that all mankind bear a fraternal resemblance and relationship to each other. And lastly, that these natural brethren are bound together by the reciprocal obligations of friendship and affection, as well as social rights. Since we are agreed, therefore, that these principles are correct, how can we, with any consistency, separate from nature that law and justice, which are her moral developements?

§ 1.36 MARCUS: You are quite right, my Atticus; the argument is pretty well established. A few considerations, however, I will add, in conformity with the method of the philosophers. I do not mean the older sages of philosophy, but those modern philosophers who keep a magazine of arguments in reserve, on every imaginable topic, and who, instead of discussing questions freely and unconstrainedly, will permit us to speak only in accordance with their logical arrangements and dialectical distinctions. These gentlemen will never allow that we have done justice to our subject, unless we demonstrate that nature is just, and justice is natural, in a distinct and scientific disputation.

ATTICUS: You seem to have renounced your liberty in debate, my Cicero, and resemble a schoolman, who rather follows the authority of his predecessors, than developes his individual sentiments.

MARCUS: I am not always in this humour, Atticus. But I wish to avail myself of authorities on the present occasion, because, as you see, the main object of this whole discussion is to strengthen the foundations of our Commonwealth, to establish its forces, and to benefit its population in all their relations. I am therefore particularly anxious to avoid any inconsiderate statements or unsound arguments. Not that I expect to demonstrate my doctrine to all men, for that is impossible; but I would make my pleadings as perfect as may be, for those who maintain that justice and honour are worthy to be cultivated even for their own sake, that nothing can he properly called a good, which is not morally estimable, and that there can exist no great good whatever, which is not desirable mainly on its own account, without reference to points of interest or emolument.

§ 1.38 All the philosophers who flourished in the old Academy with Speusippus, Xenocrates, and Polemon, or those that followed Aristotle, and Theophrastus, agreeing with them in doctrine, though they might differ in their method of explaining it—whether, like Zeno, they preserved the same principles, while they changed the terms of exposition,—or whether they supported that difficult and arduous sect of Ariston, now generally scattered and confuted, which supposed, that saving virtue and vice, all things were equal and indifferent—all these have favoured the moral theory I now unfold.

§ 1.39 For the rest, who indulged their appetites and pampered their passions, pursuing some objects and avoiding others, for no other reason than their amount of gratification or annoyance, though they sometimes speak truth, as we candidly allow,—let them talk in their own gardens, and let them retire from all the political debates respecting the interests of the state, of which they know nothing, nor, indeed, care to know. As to that new academy of which Arcesilas and Carneades are the leaders, and who attack all sects and parties, we implore them not to interrupt us in our present discussion; for if they invade us on these subjects in which our minds are thoroughly familiar and resolved, they will seek their own ruin. But I, who wish rather to please, dare not excite their resentment; for in questions of this nature, we would fain proceed without any mixture of sophistry or anger; and any defects in our arguments, may surely be expiated without such fumigations as the invectives of criticism.

ATTICUS: As you use the word 'expiation,' permit me to enquire what views you entertain respecting the justice of punishment, where laws have been broken and violated. Do you think such offences against laws can be expiated without enforcing the penalty, either directly or indirectly?

MARCUS: I think not. I conceive there is no other expiation for the crimes and impieties of men. The guilty therefore must pay the penalty, and bear the punishment. The retributions they undergo are not so much those inflicted by courts of justice, which were not always in being, do not exist at present in many places, and even where established, are frequently biased and partial; but the retributions I principally intend are those of conscience. The Furies pursue and torment them, not with their burning torches, as the poets feign, but by remorse and the tortures arising from guilt. Was it the fear of punishment, and not the nature of the thing itself that ought to restrain mankind from wickedness, what, I would ask, could give villains the least uneasiness, abstracting from all fears of this kind? And yet none of them was ever so audaciously impudent, but he endeavoured to justify what he had done by some law of nature, denied the fact, or else pretended a just sorrow for it. Now if the wicked have the confidence to appeal to these laws, with what profound respect ought good men to treat them? There is the greater need, therefore, of insisting on the natural and unavoidable penalties of conscience. For if either direct punishment, or the fear of it, was what deterred from a vicious course of life, and not the turpitude of the thing itself, then none could he guilty of injustice, in a moral sense, and the greatest offenders ought rather to be called imprudent than wicked.

§ 1.41 On the other hand, if we are determined to the practice of goodness, not by its own intrinsic excellence, but for the sake of some private advantage, we are cunning, rather than good men. What will not that man do in the dark who fears nothing but a witness and a judge? Should he meet a solitary individual in a desert place, with a large sum of money about him, and altogether unable to defend himself from being robbed, how would he behave? In such a case the man whom we have represented to be honest from principle, and the nature of the thing itself, would converse with the stranger, assist him, and show him the way. But as to the man who does nothing for the sake of another, and measures every thing by the advantage it brings to himself, it is obvious, I suppose, how such a one would act; and should he deny that he would kill the man or rob him of his treasure, his reason for this cannot be that he apprehends there is any moral turpitude in such actions, but only because he is afraid of a discovery, and the bad consequences that would thence ensue. A sentiment this, at which not only learned men, but even clowns must blush.

§ 1.42 It is therefore an absurd extravagance in some philosophers to assert that all things are necessarily just, which are established by the civil laws and the institutions of the people. Are then the laws of tyrants just, simply because they are laws? If the thirty tyrants of Athens imposed certain laws on the Athenians, and if these Athenians were delighted with these tyrannical laws, are we therefore bound to consider these laws as just? For my own part, I do not think such laws deserve any greater estimation than that past during our own interregnum, which ordained, that the dictator should be empowered to put to death with impunity, whatever citizens he pleased, without hearing them in their own defence.

There can be but one essential justice, which cements society, and one law which establishes this justice. This law is right reason, which is the true rule of all commandments and prohibitions. Whoever neglects this law, whether written or unwritten, is necessarily unjust and wicked.

But if justice consists in submission to written laws and national customs, and if, as the Epicureans persist in affirming, every thing must be measured by utility alone, he who wishes to find an occasion of breaking such laws and customs, will be sure to discover it. So that real justice remains powerless if not supported by nature, and this pretended justice is overturned by that very utility which they call its foundation.

But this is not all. If nature does not ratify law, all the virtues lose their sway. What becomes of generosity, patriotism, or friendship? Where should we find the desire of benefitting our neighbours, or the gratitude that acknowledges kindness? For all these virtues proceed from our natural inclination to love and cherish our associates. This is the true basis of justice, and without this, not only the mutual charities of men, but the religious services of the gods, would become obsolete; for these are preserved, as I imagine, rather by the natural sympathy which subsists between divine and human beings, than by mere fear and timidity.

If the will of the people, the decrees of the senate, the adjudications of magistrates, were sufficient to establish justice, the only question would be how to gain suffrages, and to win over the votes of the majority, in order that corruption and spoliation, and the falsification of wills, should become lawful. But if the opinions and suffrages of foolish men had sufficient weight to outbalance the nature of things, might they not determine among them, that what is essentially bad and pernicious should henceforth pass for good and beneficial? Or why should not a law able to enforce injustice, take the place of equity? Would not this same law be able to change evil into good, and good into evil?

As far as we are concerned, we have no other rule capable of distinguishing between a good or a bad law, than our natural conscience and reason. These, however, enable us to separate justice from injustice, and to discriminate between the honest and the scandalous. For common sense has impressed in our minds the first principles of things, and has given us a general acquaintance with them, by which we connect with Virtue every honourable and excellent quality, and with Vice all that is abominable and disgraceful.

Now we must entirely take leave of our senses, ere we can suppose that law and justice have no foundation in nature, and rely merely on the transient opinions of men. We should not venture to praise the virtue of a tree or a horse, in which expression there is an abuse of terms, were we not convinced that this virtue was in their nature, rather than in our opinion. For a stronger reason, it is mainly with respect to the moral nature of things, that we ought to speak of honour and shame among men.

If opinion could determine respecting the character of universal virtue, it might also decide respecting particular or partial virtues. But who will dare to determine that a man is prudent and cautious in his moral disposition, from any external appearances. For virtue evidently lies in perfect rationality, and this resides in the inmost depths of our nature. The same remark applies to all honour and honesty, for we judge of true and false, creditable and discreditable, rather by their essential qualities, than their external relations. Thus we judge according to their intrinsic nature, that rationality of life, which is virtue, must be ever constant and perpetual, and that inconstancy must necessarily be vicious.

We form an estimate of the opinions of youths, but not by their opinions. Those virtues and vices which reside in their moral natures, must not be measured by opinions. And so of all moral qualities, we must discriminate between honourable and dishonourable by reference to the essential nature of the things themselves.

The good we commend, must needs contain in itself something commendable. For as I before stated, goodness is not a mode of opinion: it is what it is, by the force of its very essence. If it were otherwise, opinion alone might constitute virtue and happiness, which is the most absurd of suppositions. And since we judge of good and evil by their nature, and since good and evil are the true constituents of honour and shame, we should judge in the same manner all honourable and all shameful qualities, testing them by the law of nature, without prejudice or passion.

§ 1.47 But our steady attention to this moral law of nature is often too much disturbed by the dissention of men and the variation of opinions. We might perhaps obey this law of nature more exactly, if we attended more accurately to the evidence of our senses, which being absolutely natural, are less likely to be deceived by artificial objects. Those objects, indeed, which sometimes present to us one appearance, sometimes another, we term fictions of the senses; but it is far otherwise. For neither parent, nor nurse, nor master, nor poet, nor drama, deceive our senses; nor do popular prejudices seduce them. But our delusions are connected with corruption of our mental opinions. And this corruption is either superinduced by those causes of error I have enumerated, which, taking possession of the young and uneducated, betray them into a thousand perversities, or by that voluptuousness which is the mimic of goodness, implicated and interfused through all our senses—the prolific mother of all human disasters. For she so corrupts us by her bewitching blandishments that we no longer perceive that things may be essentially excellent, though they have none of this deliciousness and pruriency. (Quae natura bona sunt quia, dulcedine hac et scabie carent.)

§ 1.48 From what I have said on this subject, it may then easily be concluded, that Justice and Equity are desirable for their own sake. For all virtuous men love Justice and Equity, for what they are in themselves; and we cannot believe that such virtuous men should delude themselves by loving something which does not deserve their affection. Justice and Right are therefore desirable and amiable in themselves; and if this is true of Right, it must be true of all the moral virtues with which it is connected. What then shall we say of liberality? Is it to be exercised gratuitously, or does it covet some reward and recompense? If a man does good without expecting any recompense for his kindness, then it is gratuitous: if he does expect compensation, it is a mere matter of traffic. Doubtless, he who truly deserves the reputation of a generous and good-natured man, performs his philanthropical duties without consulting his secular interests. In the same way the virtue of justice demands neither emolument nor salary, and therefore we desire it for its own sake, because it is its own reward. And for this reason we should entertain the same estimate of all moral virtues.

§ 1.49 Besides this, if we weigh virtue by the mere utility and profit that attend it, and not by its own merit, the virtue which results will be in fact a species of vice (malitia rectissime decitur.) For the more a man's views are self-interested, the further he recedes from probity. It therefore necessarily happens, that those who measure virtue by profit, acknowledge no other virtue than this usurious vice. For who could he called benevolent, if none endeavoured to do good for the love of others? Where could we find the grateful person, if those who are disposed to gratitude could meet no benefactor disinterested enough to deserve it? What would become of sacred friendship, if we were not to love our friends for their own sake with all our heart and soul? In pursuance of this pseudo-benovelence, we must desert our friend, as soon as we can derive no further assistance from him. What can be more inhuman! But if friendship ought rather to be cultivated on its own account, for the same reason are society, equality, and justice, desirable for themselves. If this were not so, there could be no justice at all, since nothing is more opposite to the very essence of virtue than selfish interest.

What then shall we say of temperance, sobriety, continence, modesty, bashfulness, and chastity? Is it the fear of laws, or the dread of judgments and penalties, which restrain intemperance and dissoluteness? Do we then live in innocence and moderation, only to acquire a certain secular reputation? And when we blush at licentious discourse, is it only through a squeamish prudery, lest our reputation should be stained? How I am ashamed at those philosophers, who assert that there are no vices to be avoided but those which the laws have branded with infamy. Can it be said that those are truly chaste, who abstain from adultery, merely for the fear of public exposure, and that disgrace which is only one of its many evil consequences? Indeed, my dear Atticus, what can you praise or blame with reason, if you depart from that great law and rule of nature, which makes the difference between right and wrong? Shall corporal defects, if they are remarkable, shock our sensibilities, and shall those of the soul make no impression on us?—Of the soul, I say, whose turpitude is so evidently proved by its vices. For what is there more hideous than avarice, more ferocious than lust, more contemptible than cowardice, more base than stupidity and folly? Well, therefore, may we style unhappy, those persons in whom any one of these vices is conspicuous, not on account of the disgraces or losses to which they are exposed, but on account of the moral baseness of their sins. We may apply the same ethical test to those who are distinguished for their virtue. For if virtue be not the highest excellence to which we aspire, it necessarily follows that there is something better than virtue. Is it money, fame, beauty, health? All these appear of little value to us when we possess them, especially when we consider that the duration of their enjoyment is altogether uncertain. Is it that basest of all things, voluptuousness? Certainly not; for nothing gives so much dignity to virtue, as its capacity of overruling and despising all the gratifications of secular and sensual life. You see the long series of facts and arguments I have brought forward. Such is the connection between one doctrine of truth and another,—I should have proceeded further still, if I had not kept myself in check.

QUINTUS: To what point do your arguments tend, my brother?—for I would willingly go hand in hand with you through this discussion.

MARCUS: The point they bear on, is the moral end of our actions, (ad finem bonorum) to which all things are to be referred, and for the sake of which all things are to be undertaken. This subject is, however, one of great controversy, and full of debate among the learned; yet I shall some day venture to publish my opinions respecting it.

§ 1.53 ATTICUS: How can you think of such a thing, since Gellius is no longer alive?

QUINTUS: What difference does that make?

ATTICUS: More than you imagine,—since by his death your brother has lost an excellent advocate of his benevolent design of conciliating your wrangling disputants. When I was at Athens, I recollect Phaedrus told me that your friend Gellius, when he came as a proconsul into Greece, after his praetorship, assembled all the Athenian philosophers in one spot, and very learnedly favoured them with his advice that they should endeavour to come to some unanimous agreement in their controversies; that if they were so disposed, and wished to spend their lives in peace rather than discord, such an agreement might be formed; at the same time promising them his best assistance, if this scheme of mutual conciliation and concession met their views.

MARCUS: Your story is amusing enough, my Atticus, and it excited much merriment at the time; but raillery apart, I do not see so much difficulty in harmonizing the views of the ancient Academy and Zeno,—at least, on this point.

ATTICUS: How can you form such an opinion?

MARCUS: Because they differ on one point only, and agree to admiration in all the rest.

ATTICUS: What! do they contend on one point of debate only?

MARCUS: Yes. I think they have only a single issue, so far as concerns this question of morals. For the ancient Academicians are unanimously agreed that true good consists in nature, and natural order. The Stoics, on the other hand, allow of no good but honor and virtue.

ATTICUS: This is indeed a very insignificant controversy, and not sufficient to account for their general opposition.

MARCUS: That is true, but it was the thing itself on which they differed, rather than the terms.

ATTICUS: You seem rather to agree with my friend Antiochus; I will not call him my master, since I lived with him so sociably. It was he who at one time almost persuaded me to desert my Epicurean gardens, and betake myself to those of the Academy.

MARCUS: This Antiochus was a wise and clever man, and highly accomplished in his way. He was, as you know, a friend of mine; and if I could agree with him in all those respects which I shall hereafter investigate, the whole controversy might easily be settled.

ATTICUS: Why do you prosecute this enquiry?

§ 1.55 MARCUS: Because if, as Ariston of Chios pretended, there is no other good than the honourable, no other evil than the dishonourable; that all other things are altogether indifferent, and that their presence or absence are of no kind of consequence, then Zeno has departed very far from Xenocrates, Aristotle, and all the school of Plato, and there is an entire difference between them respecting a principle which influences the whole course of life. But, as Antiochus observes, though the ancients assert that honour is the sovereign good, and its antagonist the sovereign evil,—the one being according to Zeno and the Stoics, the only good, the other the only evil—they likewise account riches, health and beauty, among the advantages, commodities and conveniences of life; and poverty, grief, and pain, among its inconveniences. And therefore they in fact agree in opinion

with Xenocrates and Aristotle, though they express it by different terms. From this difference, not respecting things, but words, the controversy concerning moral ends arose. In relation to which, inasmuch as our Roman Law of the Twelve Tables granted a neutral space of five feet wide between the territories of different landlords, we will not allow the venerable estate of the Academy to be trespassed on by this crafty man: and though the Mamilian law appointed but one surveyor to determine the rights of these neutral spaces, in this ethical question all three of us will undertake to arbitrate respecting the moral ends of philosophy.

§ 1.56 QUINTUS: What then shall be our decision?

MARCUS: I think we should seek the boundaries which Socrates has laid down in relation to this question, and abide by them.

QUINTUS: There cannot be a better proposal my brother. And now I pray you let us proceed to the consideration of civil Justice and Laws, on which topics we expect you will give us some useful information, for the subject is particularly important, as I have often heard you say. And certainly we have sufficiently established the principle we have been discussing, and proved that to live according to nature, is the highest good; that is to lead a life regulated by conscience, and conformed to virtue and temperance. Thus to follow nature, and to live according to her law, and to obey all her just commands; this surely is the most lawful and virtuous mode of living. As to the discussions of philosophers, I know not whether we shall ever arrive at a decision, but we certainly shall not do so in our present conference, at least, if we prosecute our original design, and come to the practical investigation of the civil law, as established in our country.

§ 1.57 ATTICUS: I shall most willingly proceed to that part of our disquisition!

QUINTUS: Then let us defer this dispute on moral ends to some future occasion; and let us proceed to a more practical view of laws, especially since these dialectics respecting the sovereign good and evil have but little reference to our national legislation.

MARCUS: What you say, my Quintus, is most wise and excellent, but I should not have kept you so long in these preliminary doctrines, had I not thought they would throw more light than you seem to imagine on the affairs of Jurisprudence.

QUINTUS: And when you treat of this Jurisprudence, my brother, we are not so anxious to hear of the laws of Lycurgus, and Solon, and Charondas, and Zaleucus, nor our Roman Twelve Tables, and popular decrees; but I wish you to describe, in this familiar conversation, not only the laws fitted for all nations, but also the rules and maxims of conduct that may apply to individuals.

§ 1.58 MARCUS: I would to heaven, my Quintus, that what you desire were so commensurate to my ability, that it might gracefully harmonize with the subjects I discuss. But you must allow me, that since it was necessary there should be a Law, which by censuring vice and advocating virtue, becomes the source of the precepts we most need to direct us in our conduct; it is also necessary that there should be a wisdom from the love of which, the Greeks have composed the word Philosophy, which is the parent of all the fine arts; for it is beyond contradiction the richest, the brightest, and the loveliest of the gifts the gods have bestowed on us. She has taught us, among other things, the most difficult of all lessons, namely, a precept so forcible and so comprehensive, that it has been attributed not to a man, but to the God of Delphi himself, and that not without reason.

§ 1.59 For he who knows himself must be conscious that he is inspired by a divine principle. He will look upon his rational part as a resemblance to some divinity consecrated within him, and will always be careful that his sentiments, as well as his external behaviour, be worthy of this inestimable gift of God. A serious and thorough examination of all his powers, will inform him what signal advantages he has received from nature, and with what infinite help he is furnished for the attainment of wisdom. For, from his first entrance into the world, he has, as it were, the intelligible principles of things delineated on his mind, by the enlightening assistance of which, and the guidance of wisdom, he may become a good, and, consequently, a happy man.

§ 1.60 And what can be conceived more truly happy, than the state of that man, who, having attained to an exact knowledge of virtue, throws off all the indulgences of sensual appetite, and tramples on voluptuousness as a thing unbecoming the dignity of his nature—the man who is not terrified at the approach of affliction, or even at death itself—who maintains a benevolent intercourse with his friends, and under that endearing name includes the whole race of mankind, as being united together by one common nature; who preserves, in short, an unfeigned piety and reverence towards the gods, and exerts the utmost force of his rational powers to distinguish good from evil, just as we strain our eyes, in order to view a beautiful object with greater attention.

§ 1.61 When this man shall have surveyed the heavens, the earth, and the seas, studied the nature of all things, and informed himself whence they were generated, to what state they return, the time and manner of their dissolution, what parts of them are mortal and perishable, and what divine and eternal?—when he shall have attained in a great measure, the knowledge of that Being who superintends and governs them, and shall look on himself as not confined within the walls of one city, or as the member of any particular community, but as a citizen of the universe, considered as a single Commonwealth:—on such a grand representation of things as this, and on such a prospect and knowledge of nature, how well, O heavens! would such a one understand the precepts of the Pythian Apollo by knowing himself? How insignificant would he then esteem, how thoroughly would he contemn and despise, those things which by vulgar minds are held in the highest admiration.

§ 1.62 All these acquirements he would secure and guard as with a fence, by the science of distinguishing truth from falsehood, and that logical art of reasoning which teaches him to know what consequences follow from premises, and how far one proposition clashes with another. When such a person was convinced that nature designed him for society, he would not rest contented with these subtle disquisitions, but would put in practice that comprehensive eloquence, which is necessary for governing nations, enacting laws, punishing malefactors, defending the honest part of mankind, and publishing the praises of great men. He would likewise use his persuasive eloquence to recommend salutary maxims to his countrymen, to rouse them to the practice of virtue, and turn them from wickedness, to comfort the afflicted, and, in fine, by his writings, to immortalize the wise consultations and noble actions of the prudent and brave, and to punish the shame and infamy of wicked men. So many excellent capacities will be found in man, by those who desire to know themselves, of all which Wisdom is the parent and director.

§ 1.63 ATTICUS: You have made a very sublime and just eulogium on self-knowledge. But how do you mean your remarks to bear?

MARCUS: In the first place, my Atticus, I mean them to bear on those jurisprudential topics which we shall hereafter discuss, which are well nigh as important as the preceding. For these moral principles we have already developed, would not be so grand and so interesting, if their practical consequences were not full of sublimity and beauty. And for the rest, I prosecute this enquiry with pleasure, and I trust with fairness; for law is my favourite study, and since it has made me all that I am, I cannot with any conscience pass it by without due panegyrics.

ATTICUS: So indeed it seems, if I may judge by your practice. And I commend you for it,—it is but proper to bestow all the praises we can on the topics under discussion.

§ 2.1 SECOND BOOK.

ATTICUS: Do you feel inclined, since we have had walking enough for the present, and have arrived at a new period of our discussion, to vary our situation. If you do, let us pass over to the island which is surrounded by the Fibrenus, for such, I believe, is the name of the other river, and sit down while we prosecute the remainder of our discourse?

MARCUS: I like your proposal. That is the very spot I generally select when I want a place for undisturbed meditation, or uninterrupted reading or writing.

ATTICUS: In truth, now I am come to this delicious retreat, I cannot see too much of it. Would you believe, that the pleasure I find here makes me almost despise the magnificent villas, the marble pavements, and the sculptured palaces? Who would not smile at the artificial canals which our great folks call their Niles and Euripi, after he had seen these beautiful streams? Just as you referred all things to Nature in our recent conversation on Justice and Law, you seek to preserve her domination, even in those things which are constructed to recreate and amuse the mind. I was therefore most agreeably surprised, since your letters and your verses had led me to expect nothing better in this neighbourhood than hills and rocks, to find it so delightfully ornamented by all the decorations of art. My present wonder is, how, when you retire from Rome, you condescend to rusticate in any other spot.

§ 2.3 MARCUS: I acknowledge that when I can escape for a few days, especially in this delectable season, I usually come here, on account of the beauty of the scenery, and the salubrity of the air; but these vacations occur not very often. There is one reason, however, why I am so fond of this Arpinum, which does not apply to you.

ATTICUS: Prithee, what reason is that?

MARCUS: Because, to confess the truth, it is my native place, and my brother's, for here indeed, descended from a very ancient race, we first saw the day. Here was our altar, here our ancestry, and here still remains many vestiges of our family. Besides, this villa which you behold in its present form, was originally constructed under my father's superintendence; for having very infirm health, he spent the later years of his life here, engaged in literary pursuits. At the time of my birth, my grandfather also lived here, and resided according to the olden custom, in that little villa, like another Curius on his Sabine farm. There is, therefore, an indiscribable sympathy which attaches me to the spot; it pervades my soul and sense with a peculiar fascination, whenever I reside here. Even the wisest Ulysses was not wholly exempt from a similar weakness, for Homer tells us that he renounced immortality, that he might once more re-visit his beloved Ithaca.

§ 2.4 ATTICUS: I would not condemn a sentiment which appears so rational; I myself have caught the same infection, and I feel that my love for this house and neighbourhood increases, when I remember that you were born here. I cannot tell you how this affection arises, but certainly we cannot behold, without emotion, the spots where we find traces of those who possess our esteem or admiration. For my own part, if any thing attaches me to Athens, it is not so much the accumulation of a multitude of invaluable antiques, as the rememberance of great men, whom I represent to myself as living, reposing there, and discoursing there. Even their very tombs attract my deepest attention. I therefore leave you to imagine how warm is the affection you have imparted to me for your native country.

MARCUS: That being the case, I am very glad that I have brought you here, and shown you my cradle.

ATTICUS: And I am still more pleased at having seen it. But what were you going to say just now, when you called this Arpinum the true country of yourself and your brother Quintus? Have you more than one country, or any other than that Roman Commonwealth in which we have a similar interest? In that sense, the true country of the philosophic Cato would not have been Rome, but Tusculum.

MARCUS: In reply to your question, I should say, that Cato, and municipal citizens like him, have two countries, one, that of their birth, and the other, that of their choice. Cato being born at Tusculum, was elected a citizen of Rome, so that a Tusculan by extraction, and a Roman by election, he had, besides his native country, a rightful one. So among your Athenians, before Theseus urged them to quit their rural territories, and assembled them at Athens, those that were natives of Sunium, were reckoned as Sunians and Athenians at the same time. In the same way, we may justly entitle as our country, both the place from where we originated, and that to which we have been associated. It is necessary, however, that we should attach ourselves by a preference of affection to the latter, which, under the name of the Commonwealth, is the common country of us all. For this country it is, that we ought to sacrifice our lives; it is to her that we ought to devote ourselves without reserve; and it is for her that we ought to risk and hazard all our riches and our hopes. Yet this universal patriotism does not prohibit us from preserving a very tender affection for the native soil that was the cradle of our infancy and our youth.

Therefore I will never disown Arpinum as my country, at the same time acknowledging that Rome will always secure my preference, and that Arpinum can only deserve the second place in my heart.

§ 2.6 ATTICUS: It was not then without reason, that Pompey said, when he pleaded conjointly with you the cause of Ambius, that the Commonwealth owed great gratitude to this village for having given it two of its preservers. For my part, I quite agree with you, that your native place may be called your country, no less correctly than the Commonwealth of Rome. But here we are, arrived in your favourite island. How beautiful it appears! How bravely it stems the waves of the Fibrenus, whose divided waters lave its verdant sides, and soon rejoin their rapid currents! The river just embraces space enough for a moderate walk, and having discharged this good-natured office, and secured us an arena for disputation, it hastily precipitates itself into the Liris; where, like those who ally themselves to patrician families, it loses its obscure name, and gives the waters of the Liris a greater degree of coolness.

For I have never found water much colder than this, although I have seen a great number of rivers;—and I can hardly bear my foot in it when I wish to do what Socrates did in Plato's Phaedrus.

§ 2.7 MARCUS: You justly commend the Liris, but my brother Quintus often tells me that your river Thyamis in Epirus is nothing inferior to it in beauty.

QUINTUS: Doubtless you will acknowledge that nothing on earth equals the beauties of Atticus's Amaltheum and its plane trees. But will it be agreeable to you, that we should repose here in the shade, and renew the subject which has been interrupted?

MARCUS: You have a wonderful knack of interrogation, my Quintus!—I thought that we had done with the question; but you are not a man to waive your claims.

QUINTUS: Pray begin, then; for all this day is devoted to hearing you.

MARCUS: Let us begin, then, "with great Jupiter," as I said in my translation of Aratus.

ATTICUS: Wherefore this exordium?

MARCUS: Because we cannot do better than commence, by invoking Him and the other gods.

QUINTUS: There can be no objection to this: it is but decent and proper.

§ 2.8 MARCUS: Let us, then, once more examine, before we descend to particulars, what is the essence and moral obligation of law; lest, when we come to apply it to its subordinate relations, we should not exactly understand each other for want of explanation; and lest we should be ignorant of the force of those terms which are usually employed in jurisprudence.

QUINTUS: This is a very necessary caution, and the proper method of seeking truth.

MARCUS: This, then, as it appears to me, hath been the decision of the wisest philosophers; that law, was neither excogitated by the genius of men, nor is it any thing discovered in the progress of society; but a certain eternal principle, which governs the entire universe; wisely commanding what is right, and prohibiting what is wrong. Therefore, that aboriginal and supreme law is the Spirit of God himself; enjoining virtue, and restraining vice. For this reason it is, that this law, which the gods have bestowed on the human race, is so justly applauded. For it is the reason and mind of Wisdom, urging us to good, and deterring us from evil.

QUINTUS: You have already touched on this topic. But before you come to treat of civil laws, endeavour to explain the force and power of this divine and celestial law, lest the torrent of custom should overwhelm our understanding, and betray us into the vulgar method of expression.

MARCUS: From little children have we learned, my Quintus, such phrases as this, that a man "appeals to justice, and goes to law" and a great many municipal laws have we heard mentioned; but we should not understand that such commandments and prohibitions have sufficient moral power to make us practise virtue and avoid vice.

The moral power of law, is not only far more ancient than these legal institutions of states and peoples, but it is coeval with God himself, who beholds and governs both heaven and earth. For it is impossible that the divine mind should exist without reason; and divine reason must necessarily be possessed of a power to determine what is virtuous and what is vicious. Nor, because it was nowhere written, that one man should maintain the pass of a bridge against the enemy's whole army, and that he should order the bridge behind him to be cut down, are we therefore to imagine that the valiant Cocles did not perform this great exploit, agreeably to the laws of nature and the dictates of true bravery. Again, though in the reign of Tarquin there was no written law concerning adultery, it does not therefore follow that Sextus Tarquinius did not offend against the eternal law when he committed a rape on Lucretia, daughter of Tucipitinus. For, even then he had the light of reason deduced from the nature of things, that incites to good actions and dissuades from evil ones. And this has the force of a law, not from the time it was written, but from the first moment it began to exist. Now, this existence of moral obligation is coeternal with that of the divine mind. Therefore the true and supreme law, whose commands and prohibitions are equally infallible, is the right reason of the Sovereign Deity.

QUINTUS: I grant you, my brother, that whatever is the just is always the true law; nor can this true law either be originated or abrogated by any written enactments.

MARCUS: Therefore, as the Divine Mind, or reason, is the supreme law, so it exists in the mind of the sage, so far as it can be perfected in man. With respect to civil laws, which differ in all ages and nations, the name of law belongs to them not so much by right as by the favour of the people. For every law which deserves the name of a law ought to be morally good and laudable, as we might demonstrate by the following arguments. It is clear, that laws were originally made for the security of the people, for the preservation of cities, for the peace and benefit of society. Doubtless, the first legislators persuaded the people that they would write and publish such laws only as should conduce to the general morality and happiness, if they would receive and obey them. Such were the regulations, which being settled and sanctioned, they justly entitled Laws. From which we may reasonably conclude, that those who made unjustifiable and pernicious enactments for the people, counteracted their own promises and professions; and established any thing rather than laws, properly so called, since it is evident that the very signification of the word law, comprehends the essence and energy of justice and equity.

I would therefore interrogate you on this point, my Quintus, like our inquisitive philosophers. If a state wants something, wanting which it is reckoned no state, must not that something be something good? (*Quaero igitur a te Quinte, sicut illi solent,—quo si civitas careat, ob eam ipsam causam quod eo careat, pro nihilo habenda sit, id est ne numerandum in bonis?*)

QUINTUS: A very great good.

MARCUS: Now a state which has no law, is it not for that reason to be reckoned no state?

QUINTUS: We must needs say so.

MARCUS: We must therefore reckon law among the very best things.

QUINTUS: I entirely agree with you.

MARCUS: If then in the majority of nations, many pernicious and mischievous enactments are made, as far removed from the law of justice we have defined as the mutual engagements of robbers, are we bound to call them laws? For as we cannot call the recipes of ignorant empirics, who give poisons instead of medicines, the prescriptions of a physician, we cannot call that the true law of the people, whatever be its name, if it enjoins what is injurious, let the people receive it as they will. For law is the just distinction between right and wrong, conformable to nature, the original and principal regulator of all things, by which the laws of men should be measured, whether they punish the guilty or protect the innocent.

QUINTUS: I quite agree with you, and think that no law but that of justice should either be proclaimed as a law or enforced as a law.

§ 2.14 MARCUS: Then you regard as nullable and voidable the laws of Titius and Apuleius, because they are unjust.

QUINTUS: You may say the same of the laws of Livius.

MARCUS: You are right, and so much the more, since a single vote of the senate would be sufficient to abrogate them in an instant. But that law of justice, which I have explained can never be rendered obsolete or inefficacious.

QUINTUS: And, therefore, you require those laws of justice the more ardently, because they would be durable and permanent, and would not require those perpetual alterations which all injudicious enactments demand.

MARCUS: Certainly, if I could get you both to agree with me. But Plato, that wisest philosopher, that gravest prince of literature, who first composed his Commonwealth, and afterwards his *Treatise on the Laws*, induces me to follow his illustrious example, and to proclaim the praises of law, before I begin to recite its regulations. Such likewise, was the practice of Zaleucus and Charondas, when they wrote their laws, not for literary amusement, but for the benefit of their country and their fellow-citizens. And in this conduct, they were emulated by Plato, who considered that it was the property of law, to persuade as well as compel.

§ 2.15 QUINTUS: What, do you venture to cite Zaleucus, when Timaeus denies that he ever existed?

MARCUS: But Theophrastus, an author quite as respectable, and many think more so, corroborates my opinion. His fellow-citizens too, my clients, the Locrians, commemorate him; but whether he was or was not, is of no great consequence to our argument: we only speak from tradition.

Let this, therefore, be a fundamental principle in all societies, that the gods are the supreme lords and governors of all things,—that all events are directed by their influence and wisdom, and that they are loving and benevolent to mankind. They likewise know what every person really is; they observe his actions, whether good or bad; they discern whether our religious professions are sincere and heart-felt, and are sure to make a difference between good men and the wicked.

§ 2.16 When once our minds are confirmed in these views, it will not be difficult to inspire them with true and useful sentiments,—such as this, that no man should be so madly presumptuous as to believe that he has either reason or intelligence, if he does not believe that the heaven and the world possess them likewise, or in other words, that there is no Supreme Mind which keeps the universe in motion. The presumption is the more excessive in man, who with his best philosophy, can hardly understand what the universe means.

In truth, we can scarcely reckon him a man, whom neither the regular courses of the stars, nor the alternations of day and night, nor the temperature of the seasons, nor the productions that nature displays for his use, do not urge to gratitude towards heaven.

As the beings furnished with reason are incomparably superior to those who want it, and we cannot say, without impiety, that any thing transcends the universal Nature, we must therefore confess that divine reason is contained within her. Who will dispute the utility of these sentiments, when he shall reflect how many cases of the greatest importance are decided by oaths; how much the sacred rites performed in making treaties tend to assure peace and tranquility; also, what numbers the fear of divine punishment has reclaimed from a vicious course of life; and how sacred the social rights must be in a society where a firm persuasion obtains of the immediate intervention of the immortal gods, both as witnesses and judges of our actions? Such is the preamble of the law, to use the expression of Plato.

§ 2.17 QUINTUS: You are right, my brother; I am pleased to find, however, that you take an original view of the subject, and often correct the mistakes of this philosopher, for nothing can less resemble his opinions, than what you have just now asserted, even in this preamble. I see little conformity between you, excepting in the style, which you imitate exactly.

MARCUS: I should be very glad of it, if such imitation were possible. As to his sentiments, it would be easy enough to explain them by means of paraphrases and illustrations—surely this would not be difficult to any scholar who would undertake such a task. But with regard to the thought, whatever I compose, unless it be an acknowledged quotation, I would wish it to be my own, for what merit is there in saying nearly the same thing, in nearly the same words?

QUINTUS: I entirely agree with you; for as you have justly remarked, your discourse ought to be your own. Begin, then, if you will do us the favour, and expound the Laws of Religion.

§ 2.18 MARCUS: I will explain them as well as I can; and since this place imposes no constraint, and our conversation is familiar, I shall begin by describing the Laws of Laws.

QUINTUS: What laws be they?

MARCUS: There are certain maxims of laws, my Quintus, not so ancient as the primitive sacred laws, but still possessing greater authority, and greater antiquity too, than the common parlance of the people. These legal maxims, I shall mention with as much brevity as possible; and I shall endeavour to expound the laws, not indeed in their whole extent, for this would be infinitely laborious, but those which involve the principles and contain the sum and substance of the rest.

QUINTUS: This appears a most desirable method: let us therefore hear the

MARCUS: Such are the following;—Approach the gods with purity—appear before them in the spirit of devotion—remove riches from their temples; whoever doth otherwise shall suffer the vengeance of heaven—let no one have private gods—neither new gods nor strange gods, unless publicly acknowledged, are to be worshiped privately—let the temples which the fathers have constructed in the cities, be upheld—let the sacred chapels and consecrated groves in country places be protected—let the customs of the fathers be preserved in the families—let the gods who have always been accounted celestial be worshipped, and those, gods likewise who have merited celestial honours by their illustrious actions, as Hercules, Bacchus, Aesculapius, Castor, Pollux and Quirinus. Let due honour be likewise paid to those virtues, by which man is exalted to heaven,—as intelligence, valour, piety, fidelity; and let temples be consecrated to them. But with regard to the vices, let no sacred sacrifices be paid to them. Let all contentions of every kind cease on the sacred festivals, and let servants enjoy them, their toils being remitted, for therefore they were appointed at certain seasons.—Let the priests duly render the public thank-offerings to heaven, with herbs and fruits, on the sacrificial days. Also, on the appointed holidays, let them offer up the cream of milk, and the sucklings; and lest the priests should commit any mistakes in these sacrifices, or the reason of these sacrifices, let them carefully observe the calendar, and the revolutions of the stars.—Let them provide those particular sacrifices which are most appropriate and agreeable to the particular deities: the Priests directing the service of some gods, the Flamens regulating the rites of others, and the Pontiffs superintending the worship of all.

Let the Vestal Virgins in the city carefully keep the sempiternal fire always burning on the public altar, and let those who are not instructed in the order of the ceremonials in these private and public ministrations, learn them from the priests. Let there be two classes of these priests, one to preside over ceremonials and sacrifices, and another to interpret the obscure predictions of the prophets, diviners, and sibyls, whenever the senate or the people require it.—Let the public Augurs, who are the interpreters of Jupiter, the best and greatest, likewise examine the presages and auspices, according to the discipline of their art. Let the priests who are conversant in auguries implore the prosperity of the vineyards and gardens, and the general welfare of the people.—Let those who give counsel in military or civic affairs, attend to the auspices, and take their measures accordingly.—Let them observe from what parts of heaven the lightnings burst forth.—Let them declare what lands, cities, and temples, are to be held free and consecrated.—Whatever things the augur declares to be unjust, wicked, vicious, and accursed, let them be forsaken as prohibited and disastrous, and whoever will not obey these divine indications, let him suffer capital punishment.

As to alliances, peace, war, truces, and the rights of ambassadors, the Fetial priests are the appropriate judges, who determine all questions relating to military affairs. The interpretation of all prodigies and portents, belongs to the Etruscans and Haruspices, if the senate seeks their advice, and these shall inform the partricians respecting the line of conduct they should pursue. Then will they learn what deities it behoves them to propitiate, and deprecate the fury of the thunderbolt against the object of its vengeance. (*Quibus divis creverint, procuranto; iidemque fulgura, atque obstita pianto*).

Let nocturnal sacrifices be interdicted to women, except those they offer according to popular custom—and let none be initiated in the mysteries except by the usual forms consecrated to Ceres, according to the Grecian ceremonials. (*Neve quem initianto, nisi ut assolet Cereri, Graeco sacro.*)

Let there be sacrifice made, (by the criminal) for crimes which cannot be expiated (by the priest), being acts of impiety,—the faults which can be expiated by the public priests, let them expiate. (*Sacrum commissum, quod neque expiari poterit, impie commissum esto—quod expiari poterit, publici sacerdotes expianto.*)

With regard to public spectacles, excepting those of the race-course and the ring, let them restrain the violence of the people, by the soothing influence of vocal and instrumental music; and let the honours of the gods be inseperable from the amusements of these diversions. Let them retain whatever is best and purest in the ancient form of worship. Except the devotees of Cybele (ideae matris famulos), to whom this privilege is allowed on certain days, let no one presume to levy rates for private emolument. Whoever purloins or robs the sacred property of the temples, let the sacreligious wretch be accounted as no better than a parricide. The divine punishment of perjury is destruction: the human penalty is infamy. With regard to incest, let the chief priests sentence it to the extremest penalty of the law.

Let not the impious man, who should render sacrifice, attempt to appease the gods by gifts and offerings. Let vows be piously performed. Whereever law is violated, let its punishments be executed. Let no private person presume to consecrate his land; and let his consecration of gold, silver and ivory, be made within the limits of moderation. Let private devotions be perpetually practised. Let the rights of the deities of the dead be punctually discharged. Let those who have past into the world of souls be considered as divinified; thus unnecessary expense and sorrow with regard to our departed friends will be reduced and diminished. (*Hos letho datos divos habento—sumptum in illos luctumque minuunto.*)

§ 2.23 ATTICUS: You have managed to include a great deal of law in a very small compass; but it seems to me, that this class of legal maxims does not much differ from the laws of Numa and our national regulations.

MARCUS: That is true enough. For since in my Treatise on the Commonwealth, Scipio argues that our ancient Roman constitution was the best of all governments, I could not but ordain similar laws for that excellent constitution which I imagine to myself.

ATTICUS: Certainly not.

MARCUS: Such then are the laws which a first-rate constitution should enforce. And if I add a few, which are not to be found in our Roman Commonwealth, yet even these formed a portion of the customs of our ancestors; customs which were maintained as religiously as the laws themselves.

§ 2.24 ATTICUS: Proceed, then, if you please, to propose these laws, that I may have the pleasure of ratifying them by a uti rogas, (so be it).

MARCUS: Perhaps, my Atticus, when you hear them, you will say something very different.

ATTICUS: I do not think so! I believe I shall entirely agree with you respecting the greater laws. And as for the minor ones, I shall concede them to you, and pass sentence accordingly.

MARCUS: Let us lose no time then.

ATTICUS: Go on,—propose such laws as you think advisable.

MARCUS: One of the legal maxims I have mentioned, states, that we should approach the gods with purity,—that is to say, with purity of mind; for this is every thing. Not that the law dispenses with purity of body,—but that we should understand the superiority of the mind over the body; and if we are attentive to the purity of our persons, we ought to be still more so to the purity of our souls. The pollutions of the body may indeed be removed by a few ablutions in a few days; but the stains of the conscience cannot be obliterated by any lapse of time, and all the rivers in the world cannot wash them out.

§ 2.25 The next legal maxim commands us to cultivate piety and to banish costliness from our temples. It signifies that piety is grateful to God, and all conceit of worldly wealth is displeasing to him. For if in our social relations we desire that distinctions of wealth and poverty should not induce us to forget the fraternal equality of men; why should we throw a stumbling block in the approaches of mortals to their Maker, by requiring costly sacrifices and offerings. Especially since nothing is more agreeable to the deity than to see the gates of worship flung open to all who would adore him, and serve him in his temples.

When the latter part of this legal maxim is added, which declares that God is not merely the judge, but the avenger of ecclesiastical abuses, the sense of religion is strengthened by the fear of immediate punishment which awaits the offender.

§ 2.26 The next law forbids individuals from worshipping private gods, or new gods, or strange gods, as this would introduce a confusion of religions, and ceremonies not known to the priesthood, and not acknowledged by the senate. Thus should the worship of the gods be conducted, if they approve of such regulations.

I think the temples of our ancestors should be maintained in our cities. In this respect I do not agree with the doctrine of the Persian Magi, by whose advice they say Xerxes set fire to the temples of the Greeks, because they enclosed between walls the gods, to whom all things are free and open, and whose appropriate temple and dwelling place is the boundless universe. The Greeks, and the Romans after them, have adopted a more rational opinion, since in order to confirm the devotion we entertain for the gods, we have allotted to them fixed mansions in our cities, no less than to our fellow-citizens. This opinion promotes religion, and has a useful moral influence on society. For according to the noble sentence of Pythagoras, "then chiefly do piety and religion flourish in our souls, when we are occupied in divine services." And according to Thales, the most renowned of the seven sages of

Greece, men should be persuaded that the "gods behold all things, and inform all things." And therefore are all men the more pure and holy when they frequent the sanctuaries of the gods, for there, in a certain sense, they have the divine images, not only impressed on their minds, but actually presented before their eyes.

§ 2.27 The same argument applies to the preservation of the sylvan fanes and sacred groves.

The religious honours, which, according to ancestorial custom, masters and servants pay to the lares in our villas and farms, are not to be abated,—(neque ea quae a majoribus prodita est, cum dominis tum famulis posita in fundi villaeque conspectu, religio larum repudianda est).

The rites of ancestors are likewise to be preserved in their families, for since the ancients approached nearest to the gods, that religion which the gods handed down to them is a tradition most worthy of memorial.

When the law commands us to render divine honours to deities that are consecrated, as having partaken of humanity, as Hercules and the rest, it indicates, that while the souls of all men are immortal, those of saints and heroes are divine.

§ 2.28 It is right also, that Mens, Pietas, Virtus, and Fides should possess the temples [temple of Mens] which are publicly dedicated to them at Rome, so that those who cultivate these admirable virtues, which are dear to all worthy men, should regard them as divine principles animating their souls.

But what is scarcely to be tolerated, is, that at Athens, they should have raised a shrine to vices, to Hubris [*contumelia*], and Anaideia [*inpudentia*], as they did at the instigation of Epimenides of Crete, after the expiation of the crime of Cylon. For if it is pious to consecrate the Virtues, it is impious to bestow the same honour on the Vices. Thus the ancient altar of Fever which stands in the Palatine and another on the Esquiline to Evil Fortune are detestable, and all things of this kind should be repudiated.

But when we forge titles according to the fancy of the poets, [...Vica Pota...] and call Jove Stator, Invictus, from the idea we conceive of his strength and power, and extol as divine principles, Safety, Honour, Wealth and Victory, we perhaps do little harm, since our minds are supported by the expectation of these excellent things. It was not amiss therefore, that Calatinus consecrated Hope.

Nor is it wrong to celebrate Daily Fortune, for she embraces all days, helping us through all. Nor even to extol *Fors* [Luck], which presides over irregular accidents; or her companion, *Respiciens* [Prosperity], which crowns us with unnumbered blessings.

§ 2.29 Then comes the order of festivals and holidays in which all men should be free, and spend their time without strife or litigation, and which afford the lower orders periods of rest and cessation from labour. We must appoint such holidays with a just reference to the seasons of the year, so that their distribution may rather facilitate than interrupt the useful labours of agriculture. And with respect to the time when the rites of sacrifice are to be offered, with the young animals appointed by law, the exact intervals of intercalation are to be accurately observed, an institution which, originating with Numa, was impaired by the negligence of subsequent pontiffs.

It is not desirable to change the regulations which the pontiffs and haruspices have made respecting the appropriate sacrifices due to each god, in respect of age and sex.

With respect to the priests, their great number and their attachment to the services of the several divinities, should enable them to explain all the ordinances and duties of religion. Now as Vesta, according to the meaning of the Greek word, which the Latins have retained, is symbolized by the perpetual fire of the city, the Vestal Virgins preside over it with the greatest propriety, that they may keep the sacred flame ever burning and inviolable, and that women may learn that the purest chastity constitutes the perfection of their nature.—(*Etsentiant mulieres in natura foeminarum, omnem castitatem peti.*)

§ 2.30 What follows, concerns not Religion only, but the general order of the state; namely, the prohibition which restrains private individuals from offering sacrifices without the superintendence of the public ministers of religion. For under a sound government, it always behoves the people to ask the counsel and authority of their chief functionaries; and the order of priests should take cognizance of every kind of orthodox religion.

Some of these priests are appointed to propitiate the gods, when offended, who preside over solemn sacrifices; and others are ordained to interpret the predictions of the prophets,—not indeed of all the prophets; for then their task would be infinite, and the secret purposes of the government would be divulged; so that those without the cabinet would become too familiar with political proceedings.

§ 2.31 One of the greatest and most important offices in the Commonwealth is that of the Augurs, conjoined as it is with the highest authority. I do not speak this from any motive of personal vanity, since I am an augur myself, but because it is an actual matter of fact. For what can be more important in respect of official dignities, than the power of dismissing the assembly of the Commons, though convoked by the chief rulers, and thus annulling their counsels and enactments? What, I say, can be more absolute domination than that by which even a single augur can adjourn any political proceeding to another day! What can be more transcendent than that authority of the augurs, by which they may command even consuls to lay down their office! What more sacred than their power of granting or refusing permission to form treaties and compacts! or their power of abrogating laws, which have not been legitimately enacted, as in the case of the Titian law, which was annulled by a decree of the pontifical college; and the Livian law, which was likewise annulled by the advice of Phillipus, who was at once consul and augur. Indeed there is no edict of the magistrates relating either to domestic or foreign affairs which can be ratified without the augur's authority.

ATTICUS: I confess that their authority is very great; but there is a warm dispute between Marcellus and Appius, two of the best augurs in our college. I have met with the books of both, and I find that one of them affirms that auspices are merely got up for the interests of the state, and the other seems to think that they really are supernatural divinations. Will you favour us with your opinion on this point?

MARCUS: For myself, I sincerely believe that there exists an art which the Greeks call Mantike, or magic; and that the flight of birds and other signs, which the augurs profess to observe, form a part of this magic. For when we grant the existence of the supreme gods, and their intellectual government of the universe, and their benignant dealings with the human race, and their power of granting us intimations of future events, I know not why we should deny the art of divination.

Besides this, the history of our Commonwealth affords us an infinite number of examples, which confirm this truth, and all kingdoms, peoples, and nations bear testimony that the predictions of augurs are wonderfully fulfilled. Thus the traditions of Polyidus, Melampus, Mopsus, Amphiaraus, Calchas, and Helenus, would not have made so much noise in the world, nor would they at this time be accredited by so many nations,—Arabians, Phrygians, Lycaonians, Cilicians and Pisidians, —unless antiquity had handed them down as true and indisputable. Nor would our Romulus have consulted the auspices before he founded Rome, nor would the name of Accius Navius have so long flourished in the memory of our citizens, if events had not justified their wonderful predictions. But doubtless this science and art of augury may vanish away by age and negligence. Therefore, for my part, I neither agree with Marcellus, who maintains that our college of augurs never was in possession of this science; nor do I agree with Claudius, who asserts that we still preserve it. For that kind of augury which prevailed among our ancestors, I think that it was sometimes used for mere political convenience; but far more often as a bona fide guide and director in critical emergencies. (*Quae mihi videtur apud majores fuisse, ut ad Reipublicae tempus nonnunquam, ad agendi consilium saepissime pertineret.*)

ATTICUS: Well, it might be so, and most probably was so,—but proceed.

MARCUS: I will, and as concisely as possible. What follows relates to the rights of peace and war; in commencing, conducting, and concluding which, justice and good faith are especially necessary. By our law we have therefore appointed the Fetial priests as public interpreters of these rights.

As to the religious duties of the Haruspices, concerning expiations and sacrifices, I think I have already said enough.

ATTICUS: I think so too, since that branch of the law relates exclusively to religious ceremonials.

MARCUS: As to what follows, my Atticus, I scarcely know in what terms it becomes me to animadvert, or you to assent.

ATTICUS: What is it?

MARCUS: The law respecting the nocturnal sacrifices of women.

ATTICUS: Oh! I assent to their suppression by all means, excepting those solemn and public sacrifices which your legal maxim permits.

MARCUS: But if we suppress the nocturnal sacrifices, what will become of the august mysteries of Iacchus, and the Eumolpidae? For we are constructing laws, not for the Romans only, but for all just and valiant nations.

ATTICUS: I think it is but courteous to except these mysteries likewise, especially as we ourselves happen to have been initiated in them.

MARCUS: With all my heart, let us except them. For it seems to me that among the many admirable and divine things your Athenians have established to the advantage of human society, there is nothing better than the mysteries by which we are polished and softened into politeness, from the rude austerities of barbarism. Justly indeed are they called initiations for by them we especially learn the grand principles of philosophic life, and gain, not only the art of living agreeably, but of dying with a better hope. But what displeases me in the nocturnal mysteries, is what the comic poets hold up to ridicule. If such licence was allowed at Rome, what abominations might be committed by the man who should carry premeditated debauchery into the mysteries, in which even a stolen glance was in ancient times a crime?

ATTICUS: Content yourself with proposing this law for Rome: do not rob the Greeks of their customs.

§ 2.37 MARCUS: Well then, let us return to our legal maxims, by which it is most diligently ordained that the clear daylight should be the safeguard of female virtue in the eyes of the multitude; and that they should only be initiated in the mysteries of Ceres, according to the Roman custom.

In reference to this topic, we have an extraordinary instance of the severity of our ancestors in the public indictment and prosecution of the Bacchanals by the senate, supported by the Consular armies. And this severity of the Roman government is not singular, since Diagondas the Theban, in the middle of Greece, suppressed all nocturnal mysteries by a perpetual prohibition. And Aristophanes, the most facetious of the old Greek comedians, so satirized the new gods and the nocturnal rites of their worship, that he represents Sabazius and other foreign deities condemned as aliens, and obliged to pack off from the city.

The public priest shall acquit by his counsel those irregularities committed by imprudence in the sacrifices, for this is pardonable. But he shall judge as scandalous and impious the audacity which would introduce new religions.

§ 2.38 With respect to public shows and amusements, they are generally exhibited either in the circus or the theatre. Let therefore corporeal contests, such as racing, boxing, wrestling, and charioteering for the palm of victory, be confined to the circus. And let dramatic recitations, with vocal and instrumental music within due limits, be practised in the theatre as by law prescribed. For I think with Plato that nothing more readily influences sentimental and susceptible minds, than the varied melodies of music; whose power of raising both good and evil passions is almost incalculable; for music can excite the depressed, and depress the excited, and augment our energies, or contract them. It would have been well for many of the Greek cities, if they had maintained the spirited and invigorating character of their ancient music; for since their music has been changed, their morals and manners have lapsed into voluptuousness and effeminacy. Whether their dispositions have been depraved by this seducing and enervating music, or whether their heroism has yielded to the temptation of other vices, certainly both their sense of honour and their sense of hearing must have been corrupt enough ere they could find pleasure in their newfangled concertos.

§ 2.39 Therefore it was, that Plato, that wisest and learnedest philosopher of Greece, so much dreaded the effects of music on his fellow-countrymen. He denied that it was possible to change the laws of music, without likewise changing the laws of manners. If I am not quite so timid as Plato with respect to the influence of music, I by no means believe that this influence is to be slighted or overlooked by the moralist or the lawyer. Without going further, let me observe the effect of that influence among our Romans. The verses of Livius and Naevius, which used to be sung with a manly simplicity and energy, are now chanted forth with all sorts of grimaces and contortions of the eyes and head, according to the variation of the airs. Ancient Greece never permitted such abuses, wisely foreseeing, that if this kind of effeminacy got possession of the citizens, it would ruin all their cities with false arts and luxurious indulgences. And therefore the stern Lacedaemon ordained that the harp of Timotheus should possess but seven chords, and that the rest should be taken away.

§ 2.40 Our next legal maxim is, that we should be conservatives, and retain whatever is best in our ancient customs, (*ut de ritibus patriis colantur optimi*): respecting which conservative principles, when the Athenians consulted the Pythian Apollo what religions they should chiefly cultivate, the oracle answered, "those which were sanctioned by their ancestors." (*Eas quae essent in more majorum*). And when the Athenians came to consult the oracle again, alleging that the customs of their ancestors were various, and they desired to know which custom they should select from the variety, the oracle replied, "the best" (*optimum*). And truly may we assert, that for the most part the best is the most ancient and nearest the gods.

We have by another legal maxim prohibited the levy of rates for private emoluments, with the exception of those that are made during a few days in honour of Cybele. Such a custom fills men's minds with superstition, and impoverishes their families. (*Stipem sustulimus, nisi eam quam ad paucos dies propriam, Idaeae matris excepimus, implet enim superstitione animos, et exhaurit domos.*)

We have awarded a due punishment for all sacriligious persons, not those only who rob a temple, but also those who rob property intrusted to a temple, which exists to a larger amount in many churches.

§ 2.41 Thus, Alexander is said to have consigned a sum of money in a sanctuary of the Solenses in Cilicia, and Cleisthenes the Athenian, a very worthy citizen, when he thought his fortune was in danger, consigned his daughters' doweries to the care of Juno, in her temple at Samos.

Respecting the law against perjury, I have nothing more to add; and with regard to the laws against incest, this is not the place to dispute.

The next legal maxim is, that reprobates should not attempt to appease the gods by offerings, till they have repented of their sins. Let such impious criminals listen to Plato, who forbids us to doubt that God must abhor the wicked, since even a good man will not receive presents from the apostate.

The next legal maxim enforces the necessity of a careful discharge of our vows towards God.

As to the punishments of those who violate the sacred rites of religion, no one will deny the propriety of such penalties. In order to confirm the execution of justice on such offenders, I need not cite the examples of those impious wretches, whose crimes and punishments are represented in the tragedies. Let us rather speak of those things which pass under our own observation. And though, in commemorating my private history, it may seem to have surpassed the usual fortune of men, yet as our present conversation is so familiar and confidential between ourselves, I will hide nothing, and I trust that what I shall say will be agreeable to the immortal gods rather than offensive.

§ 2.42 You are too well aware that all the laws of religion were infringed by certain wicked men during the period of my banishment. Our *Lares familiares* were violated, and a temple to licentiousness built on the ruins of their edifice, while he who alone could defend them was driven from their altars. Consider then, a moment, (for I need not mention names,) what was the termination of such proceedings. I, who suffered not the statue of Minerva, the guardian of our city, to be polluted by impious hands during the universal ruin of my house and property, and carried her safely from my home to the capitol, which is the home of Jupiter himself; was I not thus acting, celebrated by the judgment of the senate, Italy, and all nations as the preserver of my country?—than which nothing more glorious could happen to a mortal man.

My enemies, on the other hand, who had abominably violated the sacred rites of religion, were for the most part banished and exiled; while those who headed them in all their crimes and impieties, not only suffered degradation during life, but were denied the privilege of sepulture and funeral ceremonies.

§ 2.43 QUINTUS: Yes, my brother, you have described these events as they occurred, and we cannot feel too grateful to the gods; but we sometimes see virtue apparently unrewarded, and vice triumphant.

MARCUS: This is, because we judge not as we ought to judge, respecting divine justice. We are carried by the tide of public opinion into error, and cease to discern the true nature of things. We talk as if all the miseries of man were comprehended in death, pain of body, sorrow of mind, or judicial punishments; which, I grant, are calamitous accidents which have befallen many good men; but the sting of conscience, the remorse of guilt, is in itself an infinitely greater evil, even exclusive of the external punishments which attend it. I have seen those, who, had they not been enemies to their country, would never have been foes to me, tormented beyond description by their own bad passions; burning with concupiscence, and shuddering with terror and regret. Whatever they did they did it timorously, contemning religion, as if by so doing they could escape its penalties; and as if by corrupting men they could corrupt the gods. But I must restrain myself, and go no further in invective; for my vengeance has already been carried beyond my desire.

§ 2.44 I would only indicate, that the divine punishment of the impious is double their legal penalties; for it consists in the pang of conscience while they live, and the reported anguish of the dead; so that their chastisement may become manifest, both to the judgment and the satisfaction of the living.

§ 2.45 I agree with Plato, that private estates ought not to be consecrated. Here are his words on this subject, if I can but interpret them correctly. The earth is consecrated to all the gods, as a grand altar of worship. Therefore private individuals should not consecrate to the gods those territories which belong to them already. As to gold and silver in the cities, whether in houses or sanctuaries, this sort of property may very properly be consecrated. As to ivory, which is extracted from a dead elephant, it is an offering scarcely pure enough for the gods. Bronze and iron, the instruments of war, ought not to be consecrated in sanctuaries. With regard to wood, if any one wishes to dedicate a statute of wood to a divinity, let it be formed from a single tree. The same remark applies to the statues of stone, in common shrines, which should be constructed of one material. As to the dress of a statue, let it not be more elaborate than a woman can make it in a month. Let its colour be white, for this is most pleasing to God, as a general emblem of purity, and peculiary appropriate for sacred vestments. Let there be no colours, therefore, excepting on military decorations. With regard to offerings, the most pleasing ones we can render to the gods are birds, and other simple figures, which a painter may draw in a day; and let the other gifts have the same character of simplicity.

Such is the opinion of Plato. For my part, I am not quite so strict in my limitations, for we have to consider the present tone of public morals, and the abundance of wealth in all the articles of commerce. Besides, I suspect that agricultural industry would languish, if superstitious ceremonials were allowed unduly to interfere with the cultivation of the ground by the instruments of husbandry.

ATTICUS: I understand you; it remains for you to speak on the perpetual sacrifices and the rights of the Manes.

MARCUS: What a wonderful memory you possess, my Atticus. I had forgotten that point.

§ 2.46 ATTICUS: Very likely. I recollect these legal maxims the better, because they are associated both with the pontifical and civil law.

MARCUS: On these points, our statutes and decisions are very clear and distinct. And for my part, in this familiar conversation, whatever kind of law we have to discuss, I will treat of our civil jurisprudence with as much simplicity as possible,—in such a manner, that you may easily distinguish on what principle every legal case depends. Thus it will not be difficult for any one possessed of a moderate share of intelligence to find the rights of the question, whatever new cause of consultation shall arise, when he shall know how to refer the points of debate to their appropriate maxim.

§ 2.47 But, unhappily, our lawyers, whether for the sake of raising casuistry (*erroris objiciendi causa*) in order that they may seem to know more difficult points than they really understand—or whether, as most likely, through ignorance of the art of teaching and conveying instruction (for it is one thing to know an art, and another to teach it) our lawyers, I say, often divide a legal doctrine, which is essentially simple, into an infinite variety of technical distinctions, (*saepe quod positum est in una cognitione, id in infinita dispartiuntur*). With relation to our present topic, for instance, what a wonderful cloud of sophistries has been raised by the two Scaevolas, pontiffs both equally skilful in law! Often, says Publius the son, have I heard from my father, that no one can make a good pontiff, unless he understands the civil law. What, the whole of it? Why so? What in the world has a pontiff to do with the rights of partition walls, aqueducts, etc. Or does he mean only that part of the civil law which is connected with ecclesiastical polity? But how inconsiderable is this, with the exception of certain sacrifices, vows, holidays, burials, and things of that kind. Why then should we make these of so much importance, when the others are so insignificant?

Concerning those sacrifices, however, which have a more extensive relation to jurisprudence, we may pronounce this sentence: let them be preserved perpetually,—and let them pass by succession through families, so that, as I have stated in my maxim, the sacred rites may be constant.

§ 2.48 On this principle, the pontiffs have decided that these rites should be handed down through all generations, so that their memorial should not fail with the lives of the ancestor, and that their obligations should devolve on those who inherit the family estates. On this principle alone, which might suffice for the regulation of all relative cases, have our lawyers raised innumerable quibbles, which fill their books. They demand, forsooth, who are bound to administer these sacred rites? Common justice evidently points out the heir of the deceased; for there is no other person who more appropriately occupies the position of the departed progenitor. Next to the heir, stands the legatee, who by the death of the deceased, or by virtue of his will, sometimes takes as much as all the heirs. All this is implied in the maxim, and perfectly corresponds to its design. Thirdly, if there be no heir, the obligation attaches to him who takes the largest share of the goods of the deceased. Fourthly, if there be no heir or legatee who receives any thing, it binds the chief creditor who gains the largest share of the estate.

§ 2.49 The last person on whom the obligation of discharging the sacred rites can fall, is the debtor of the defunct, who not having discharged the debts he owed him, will stand in the same position as if he had received a legacy to an equivalent amount. It is thus, that Scaevola instructed us in many points of law, which were not so defined by our forefathers. For they regulated the whole business in the following simple terms:—A person may become liable to the obligation of discharging the sacred rites of the deceased in three ways; first, as the heir; secondly, as the legatee, who takes the greater part of the property; thirdly, as the largest creditor, in case the estate is encumbered.

§ 2.50 But we learn one thing from Scaevola the pontiff, namely, that all the new arrangements depend on a single principle, which is the wish of the priests to attach the money to the sacred rites, and they judge all festivals and ceremonies by the same rule. The Scaevolas likewise establish this regulation, which is one of their distinctions: namely, that if a due allowance is not set down in the legacy, and the legatees receive less than all the heirs, they should not be bound to discharge the sacred rites. In donations, however, they interpret the same thing in quite a different manner, and ratify whatever the ancestor shall approve in the donation of a person under his superintendence; and do not ratify whatever has been done without his approbation and participation.

§ 2.51 On such topics, a thousand little questions arise, which any one may solve by referring them to their proper maxim and principle. For instance,—if through fear of being charged with the sacred rites, a legatee took less than his legacy, and afterwards one of the heirs of this legatee claimed on his own account that portion which the legatee had relinquished, and these two sums, joined together, equal that which was bequeathed to all the heirs; then he who claimed this relinquished portion would be bound to perform the sacred rites, without encumbering his co-heirs. They determine, however, with regard to the legatee, that where the legacy is greater than can be exempted, from these rites, he may pay a part by weight and balance to the testamentary heir, so that in this case, the heir being charged, the money of the legatee is no further liable.

§ 2.52 On this point, as on many others, I should be glad if you pontiffs Scaevolas, great and talented men, as I confess you to be, would inform me why you seek to perplex the pontifical law with the subtleties of the civil law? For thus, you, in fact, supersede the simple maxims of ecclesiastical jurisprudence, by the endless technicalities of the municipal legislation. If the sacred rites are thus conjoined with pecuniary interests, they are so by your authority as pontiffs, rather than by any law of national obligation. So long, indeed, as you remain pontiffs, your pontifical jurisdiction will continue, but as you happen to be exceedingly knowing in the civil law, you may be able to elude the plainest maxims of the ecclesiastical. For instance, Publius Scaevola, Coruncanius, and other chief priests, have determined that those legatees who take only as much as all the heirs, should be bound to discharge the sacred rites.

§ 2.53 Such is the pontifical law. Now what has been added to it by the civil law?—a rule of distributions, composed with the utmost caution, in favour of the legatee, for by the deduction of a hundred sesterces, they have discovered a method of delivering the legatee from this troublesome duty. If, however, the testator omitted to make this proviso for the legatee, Mucius the pontiff and jurisconsult, has contrived a new expedient in his favour: he has but to take less than all the heirs, and he gets his acquittal. Our forefathers had stated, with admirable good sense, that those to whom the property came should discharge the sacred rites; but these pontifical gentlemen have rid them of all such obligations. As to the other quibble, it had no place in the pontifical law, and existed only in the civil code. I mean the sale by weight and balance, in order to charge the testamentary heirs, and place the business in the same condition as if the legacy had not been granted, the legatee stipulating with respect to his legacy, that he should pay over a certain sum by stipulation and so get acquitted of the sacred rights.

§ 2.54 I now come to the rights of the Manes, or ghosts of the dead—which our ancestors most wisely instituted, and most religiously observed. They therefore ordained that the people should sacrifice for the ghosts of the dead, in the month of February, then the last month in the year by the ecclesiastical calendar. Decius Brutus, however, according to the writings of Sisenna, usually discharged these ceremonials in December. When I consult my own knowledge for the reason of this proceeding, I think I discover the cause which induced Brutus to depart from the ancestorial custom. The cause that Sisenna assigns for Brutus's non-observance of this ancient institution, was his ignorance of its obligation; but it does not seem to me likely that Brutus would have so rashly neglected an institution of our ancestors, for he was a learned man, and very familiar with Accius. I therefore conclude that Brutus considered December to be the last month in the year, rather than February, which was so called when the institution was originated. He, likewise, conceived that it was a part of piety to offer very considerable sacrifices.

§ 2.55 With regard to the rite of sepulture, it is so sacred a thing that all confess it should be discharged in consecrated ground, and if possible in the country where the family of the deceased resides. Thus, in ancient times, Torquatus adjudicated respecting the Popilian family. And certainly the Denicale feasts, so called from the Latin words *de nece* (implying deliverance from death) would not have been appointed as holidays in honour of the dead, as well as other celestials, unless our ancestors who have departed this life, were believed to have past into the great assembly of divinified minds. The order of solemnizing these days, which is different from that of other public festivals, declares the ecclesiastical character of this institution, and its great sanctity and importance. It is unnecessary for us at present to explain the proceedings of families in funeral ceremonies, what kind of sacrifice should be offered to the Lares, or guardian *genii*, from the rams of the flock—how the bone which remains unconsumed must be covered with earth—how in some cases it is necessary to sacrifice a sow, when the sepulchre is to be considered as consecrated, and such minute details.

§ 2.56 It appears to me, however, that the kind of sepulture which Cyrus, according to Xenophon, solicited for himself, is the most ancient of all, for it is a kind of restitution which we make to the earth of a body, which, as a mother, she produced, and as a mother takes back to her protecting bosom. In the same manner we believe our ancient king Numa was interred in his sepulchre, near the altar of the fountain. The Cornelian family likewise used this form of burial, till a period within our own recollection. The conqueror Sylla, however, ordered the corpse of Marius to be disinterred from his grave on the banks of the Anio, impelled to this barbarous brutality by an implacable resentment, which he would not have indulged if he had been as wise as he was vehement. Perhaps it was through fear that the same accident might happen to himself, that he ordered that his body should be burned after his death,

§ 2.57 A custom he was the first to introduce in the patrician family of the Cornelii. For in the epitaph on Scipio Africanus, Ennius says,

Here lies the body

And the word lies is only applied in this way to them who are buried in sepulchres; though perhaps tombs should not be entitled sepulchres till the last rites have been consummated, and the corpse consumed by fire.

The verb to inhume which is now commonly applied to the burial of the deceased, is most appropriate to those corpses that are interred after being burned. The pontifical law proves this usage, for before the ground is thrown over them, the spot where the body is burned is not consecrated. When the earth is thrown over the corpse, then it is inhumed, and the tomb is called a sepulchre, and many religious rites are performed in order to consecrate it. So Publius Mucius determined with regard to a person killed in a ship, and then cast into the sea, that his family was pure from any charge of neglect to the deceased, inasmuch as no bone remained on the earth, in which case his heir must have sacrificed a sow to his manes. If, on the contrary, a bone had remained on the earth, he considered that fasts should be appointed during three days, and that a sow should likewise be sacrificed, if the deceased had died in the sea.

§ 2.58 ATTICUS: I am well aware of these rules of the pontifical statutes; but what do our civil laws say?

MARCUS: Little enough on this subject, my Atticus, and I expect you are acquainted with it already. The civil regulation has less regard to the religious ceremonials than to the rights of sepulchres. A law of the Twelve Tables determines that a dead person shall neither be buried nor burned within the city, I suppose on account of the danger of fire. But the addition of this disjunctive nor burned, indicates, that the corpse which is burned is not so appropriately consigned to burial as to inhumation.

ATTICUS: How is it, that notwithstanding this law of the Twelve Tables, so many of our great men have been buried in the city?

MARCUS: I believe, my Atticus, that this privilege was granted before this law was made, to certain heroic worthies, as Publicola and Tubertus, on account of their virtue, and that their descendents have succeeded to this privilege, though it is an exception to the law. Some others may since have gained this privilege, like Caius Fabricius, whose virtue has in some sense made them free of the laws. The civil law, in all other cases, forbids burials in the city, and the Pontifical College has decreed that it is unlawful to raise a sepulchre in the public places.

You know the Temple of Honour, outside the Colline gate. We learn from tradition, that there was in ancient times an altar on the spot; and it appears from a medal discovered there, on which was inscribed, the name "Honour." that this was the reason why that temple was so dedicated. But since there were many sepulchres in the neighbourhood, they were ploughed up when the city was enlarged. For the Pontifical College ordained that public places could not be bound by private consecrations.

§ 2.59 Another provision we find in the Twelve Tables, intended to obviate the superfluous expenses and extravagant ceremonials of funerals, almost literally translated from the laws of Solon. "*Ne facito rogum ascia ne polito.*" Never carve and polish a funeral pile. You recollect what follows, for we learned the Twelve Tables when schoolboys, as an indispensable lesson, which, by-the-bye, no one attends to now-a-days. Let extravagance, therefore, be diminished to three suits of mourning, with purple bands, and ten flute players. Excessive lamentations are also to be prohibited by this rule,—Let not the women tear their cheeks or make the lessus or funeral wailings.

Those ancient interpreters of our laws, Sextus, Aelius, and Lucius Accilius, have said they could not understand this regulation, but that they suspected it referred to some peculiar funeral ceremonials. Aelius defines the word 'lessus' to be a kind of lugubrious ejaculation, or shriek, which I think likely enough, since Solon's law likewise forbids such lamentations. These rules are very commendable, and equally practicable by the rich and poor, and they are eminently conformable to nature, who sweeps away by mortality all the distinctions of fortune.

§ 2.60 The Twelve Tables, have likewise abridged those other funeral pomps, which tend to augment a vain and unavailing sorrow. For they thus declare,—Do not collect the bones of the dead, when their funerals are over. An exception is made with regard to those who die in battle, or in a foreign land. Besides these laws, there are others with regard to unction, which forbid a servile embalming of the corpse, and funeral banquets and wakes. These abuses are justly abrogated, which would not have been abrogated had they not been abuses.

Among the prohibitions are likewise comprised expensive respersions, large crowns, and censers of perfume.

It is certain, however, that the ornament of merit may sometimes belong to the dead, because the law enjoins that such a crown should be placed without fraud on the deceased, who has deserved it by his virtue, and on his nearest relation.

I believe there was also a rule that many obsequies should not be celebrated, or many funeral processions arranged for any one deceased.

And since, there was a general law, that gold should not be buried with the dead—another regulation contained this humane exception; if the teeth of the deceased were fastened with gold, the corpse should be buried or burned without taking it away. From which expression we might deduce another argument, that burial and burning were often quite unconnected.

§ 2.61 Beside these, there are two laws respecting sepulchres, one of which relates to the houses that have family vaults attached, and the other to the family vaults themselves. One prohibits the erection of a funeral pile or pyre nearer than sixty feet to a neighbour's house, without its proprietor's consent, for fear of conflagration. The other ordained, that the sepulchre and its vestibule should not be subject to usucaption, and thus defends the rights of sepulchres.

These regulations we find in the Twelve Tables, and indeed they are very conformable to nature, which is the rule of law. The other portion relates to customs—how funerals should be announced; whether games should be allowed; whether the master of the ceremonies shall employ a herald and lictors;

§ 2.62 whether the praises of the honorable dead shall be commemorated in a panegyric; whether the elegiac songs shall be accompanied by flutes, so as to form dirges, by which name Gracchus designated funeral lamentations.

QUINTUS: I am delighted that our laws are so far conformable to nature, and above measure pleased with the wisdom of our ancestors.

MARCUS: Yet I believe, my Quintus, that some further limitation should be made to the funeral pomps and ceremonials. You may see in the funeral of Figulus to what an excess these vanities were carried.

QUINTUS: I think there was formerly far less ambition for this kind of extravagance than at present prevails, as many examples of funeral frugality and simplicity are extant in the records of our ancestors.

MARCUS: At least our legal interpreters inform us, that the chapter of the law which forbids profuse and excessive ceremonials in the funeral rites of the dead, likewise condemns the superfluous magnificence of sepulchres. And we cannot believe that this important subject should have escaped the attention of our wisest legislators. They say that the custom of interring the dead in the Greek mode, began at Athens in the time of Cecrops. And that immediately after such interments, the next relatives, when they had cast the earth over the dead, scattered the seeds of vegetables over the spot; that, having like a benignant mother, taken her lifeless son to her bosom, by the expiation of the seed she should again bear fruit for the living. Then followed the festivals, which the relatives attended, crowned with flowers; and in these festivals they pronounced the eulogies on the deceased, if his virtues were worthy of commendation; for it was reckoned impious to lie on such occasions, and thus the ceremony terminated.

§ 2.64 In process of time, as Demetrius Phalereus assures us, the funerals became sumptuous, and the elegiac lamentations were extravagantly multiplied. These abuses were prohibited by Solon's law, which our Decemvirs have translated almost word for word in our Twelve Tables. Our rule respecting the three suits of mourning, and other customs were thus derived from Solon's regulation; and that edict respecting the dirges is expressed in his precise phrases.—Let not the women tear their cheeks, nor indulge their wailing at funerals. (*Mulieres genas ne radunto, neve lessum funeris ergo habento*).

There is nothing more to be remarked in Solon's law respecting funerals, except, that he forbids the injury of sepulchres, or the disturbance of the dead. He makes it penal for any one to violate, dilapidate, or impair any grave, which he calls a τύμβον, or monument or column. But after some time, the extravagance of the mausoleums we see in the Ceramicus, gave occasion to that law which prohibits private persons from erecting any sepulchre more elaborate than ten men can construct in three days.

§ 2.65 Nor was it permitted to adorn them with sculpture, nor to place the statues they call Herms around them; nor to pronounce the panegyrics of the dead, excepting when the obsequies were public, and the constituted officer was duly employed. The eulogies of men and women were likewise forbidden, that the lamentations might be diminished; for such convocations on melancholy occasions tend to augment unavailing sorrow.

§ 2.66 Therefore Pittacus expressly forbade any from attending the funerals of those that were strangers to them. But as the same Demetrius informs us, the magnificence of funeral processions and ceremonials revived anew, so as nearly to equal our present Roman extravagances; these, Demetrius restrained by a wholesome law; for he was not only, as you are aware, a very learned man, but a most experienced citizen, devoted to the preservation of the state. He therefore diminished the sumptuosity of funerals, not only by penalties, but by a limitation of time; as he commanded that they should be performed before sun-rise. He also established a rule of moderation for all new sepulchres—for he would not allow any edifice over the dead, save a little column, three cubits high, or a tomb-stone, or tablet; and he appointed a regular magistrate to superintend these observances.

§ 2.67 Such, my Atticus, were the laws enforced among your Athenians. But let us see what says Plato, who allots to the expounders of religion the charge of regulating funerals, of which we sometimes take cognizance in our civil courts. These are his words respecting sepulchres:—

"Do not use, as a burial place, any portion of land which is either cultivated, or which may be so; but such a soil as nature has adapted for receiving the bodies of the dead, without detriment to the interests of the living. As to the field, which is capable of bearing fruit, and nourishing us with its maternal exuberance of vegetable stores, let us by no means injure it either living or dead.

§ 2.68 And let no sepulchre be built to a greater elevation than five men can raise in five days; nor let a tablet be made any larger than is required for the reception of an epitaph on the deceased, in four heroic verses,"; (which, our Ennius says, is quite long enough.)

We have therefore the authority of the illustrious Plato in our favour. He likewise limits the funeral expenses by the fortune of the family, from one mina to five. He then repeats what he had before said respecting the immortality of the soul, and the tranquility of the good after death, and the punishment of the wicked.

§ 2.69 I have now, I believe, sufficiently explained all the laws which relate to religious rites.

QUINTUS: You have, my brother, and most copiously too; but prithee proceed to the other branch of our subject.

MARCUS: It is my intention to do so; and since you urge me to these discussions, I will endeavour to bring our argument to a conclusion, and if possible, in the course of the day. For I find my predecessor Plato did the same, and got through each legal disquisition in a summer day's conference. I will, therefore, try to imitate him, and will next speak of magisterial laws; for after those of religion, the state hath nothing more important.

ATTICUS: Proceed, then, and in the same order and method you have discussed the sacred laws, endeavour to illustrate our civil regulations.

§ 3.1 THIRD BOOK

MARCUS: I shall, therefore, emulate that divine man who has inspired me with such admiration, that I eulogize him perhaps oftener than is necessary.

ATTICUS: You mean Plato.

MARCUS: The very man, my Atticus.

ATTICUS: Indeed you do not exaggerate your compliments, nor bestow them too frequently, for even my Epicurean friends, who lavish all their praises on Epicurus, still allow me to love Plato as much as I like.

MARCUS: They do well to grant you this indulgence, for what can be so suitable to the elegance of your taste as the writings of Plato?—who in his life and manners effected that most difficult combination of gravity and politeness.

ATTICUS: I am glad I interrupted you, since you have availed yourself of an opportunity of giving this splendid testimonial of your esteem; but let us pursue our subject.

MARCUS: Let us begin, then, with praising our civil laws, with all the commendations they truly and appropriately deserve.

ATTICUS: It is but fair, since you paid the same preliminary compliment to our ecclesiastical jurisprudence.

MARCUS: You are aware, then, that the proper characteristic and duty of magistrates, is to superintend and prescribe all the just and useful regulations of the law. For as the law is set over the magistrate, even so are the magistrates set over the people. And, therefore, it may be said "that the magistrate is a speaking law, and the law a silent magistrate."

Now it is self-evident, that nothing can be more conformable to justice and natural conscience, which to me appear perfectly congenial, than that legal authority, without which, neither house, nor commonwealth, nor nation, nor mankind itself, nor the entire nature of things in this immeasurable universe, could consist. For this universe is obedient to God, and land and sea are submissive to the universe; and human life depends on the just administration of the laws of order.

But to come to considerations nearer home, and more familiar to us, all ancient nations have been under the dominion of kings (omnes antiquae gentes regibus quondam paruerunt). Which kind of authority was at first conferred on the wisest and justest men. And this rule mainly prevailed in our own Commonwealth, as long as the regal power lasted. Afterward, the authority of kings was handed down to their descendants, which remains to this day, in those that reign over nations. And even among those to whom the regal domination was distasteful, though they desired to disclaim their submission to the laws of a monarch, they by no means sought to be emancipated from all laws.

For ourselves, then, as we propose laws for a free people, such as we approved in that best kind of Commonwealth, concerning which we wrote our Six Books, we shall now endeavour to accommodate our laws to that constitutional government we there set forth and illustrated.

§ 3.5 It is clear, then, that magistrates are absolutely necessary to a state, since, without their prudence and diligence, there would be nothing but confusion and anarchy. Their lawful authority is therefore to be determined in the legislation of every Commonwealth. But it is not enough to prescribe them a rule of domination, unless we likewise prescribe the citizens a rule of obedience. For in order to command well, we should know how to submit; and he who submits with a good grace will some time become worthy of commanding. It is desirable therefore, that he who obeys may hope that some day he will be capacitated for command, and that he who commands should bear in mind that ere long he may be called to the duty of submission.

We would not, however, limit ourselves to requiring from the citizens submission and obedience towards their magistrates; we would also enjoin them by all means to honour and love their rulers, as Charondas prescribes in his code. Our Plato likewise declares that they are of the race of the apostate Titans, exiled from heaven for their seditions, who oppose their legitimate magistrates. These points being granted, we will, with your permission, advance to the examination of the magisterial laws.

§ 3.6 ATTICUS: There cannot be a better arrangement of your topics.

MARCUS: I will, therefore, cite a few of the legal maxims that bear on this branch of laws. Let all authorities be just, and let them be honestly obeyed by the people without hesitation. Let the magistrate restrain disobedience and sedition in citizens, by fine, imprisonment, and corporal chastisement. If there be an equal or greater power, and the people think the adjudication unjust, let them lawfully appeal thereto. If the magistrate shall have decided, and past sentence illegally, let there be a public appeal in a higher Court respecting the penalty and fine imposed.

With respect to the army, and the generals that command it by martial law, there should be no appeal from their authority. For the will of the general should have the force of absolute law, at least in time of war.

As to the minor magistrates, let there be such a distribution of their legal duties, that each may more effectively superintend his own department of justice. In the army let some, as military tribunes, command those that are subject to them. In the city, let others be appointed as superintendents of the public treasury. Let some devote their attention to the prison discipline, and capital punishments. Let others supervise the public mintage of gold, and silver, and copper. Let others judge of suits and arbitrations; and let others carry the orders of the senate into execution. Let there likewise be aediles, curators of the city, the provisions, and the public games, and let these offices be the first steps to higher promotions of honour.

Let the censors take a census of the people, according to age, race, family, and property. Let them have the inspection of the temples, the streets, the aqueducts, the rates, and the customs. Let them distribute the citizens, according to their tribes, fortunes, ages, and ranks. Let them keep a register of the equestrian and plebeian orders. Let them impose a tax on celibates. Let them guard the morals of the people. Let them permit no scandal in the senate. Let the number of such censors be two. Let their magistracy continue five years. Let the other magistrates be annual, but their offices themselves should be perpetual.

Let the praetor be judge of the law in private actions, with power of passing sentence—he is the proper guardian of civil jurisprudence. Let him have as many colleagues, of equal power, as the senate think necessary, and the commons allow him. Let two magistrates be invested with sovereign authority, and be entitled praetors, judges, or consuls, in respect of presiding, judging, or counselling, according to the nature of the case. Let them have absolute authority over the army, for the safety of the people is the supreme law.

§ 3.9 This magistracy should not be determined in less than ten years—regulating the duration by the annual law. When a considerable war is undertaken, and discord is likely to ensue among the citizens, let a single supreme magistrate be appointed, who shall unite in his own person the authority of both consuls, if the senate so decrees, for six months only. When such a magistrate has been proclaimed under favourable auspices, let him be as a prince of the people. Let him have for a colleague, a praetorial patrician, as a judge of the law. But when such dictators are created over the consuls, let not the other magistracies be suppressed or vacated.

§ 3.10 Let the auspices be observed by the senate, and let those they authorize to elect the consuls in the comitia, proceed according to the established ceremonials.

Let the governors, generals, and lieutenants, leave the city whenever the senate or the people decree their retirement. Let all wars be just, and justly prosecuted. Let allies be spared, and our armies restrained from all unnecessary violence, that the glory of our country may be augmented. Then shall our soldiers return home with honour. Let ambassadors also direct their efforts to the service of the state, rather than their selfish interests.

Let ten tribunes be elected as magistrates of the people, to protect them against oppression; let their prohibitions and their adjudications be established, and their persons considered inviolable, so that tribunes may never be wanting to the people. Let all magistrates possess their auspices and jurisdictions, and let the senate be composed of these legitimate authorities. Let its ordinances be absolute, and let its enactments be written and enrolled, unless an equal or greater authority disannul them. Let the order of the senators be free from reproach and scandal, and let them be an example of virtue to all.

In the creation of magistrates, the judgment of the accused, and the reception or rejection of laws, when suffrages are employed,). If any question occur out of the established jurisdiction of the magistrates, let another magistrate be appointed by the people, whose jurisdiction shall expressly extend thereto. Let the consul, the praetor, the censor, and he to whom the senate has committed the election of consuls, have full liberty to treat both with the senate and the people, and endeavour to reconcile the interests of all parties. Let the tribunes of the people likewise have free access to the senate, and advocate the interests of the people in all their deliberations. Let a just moderation predominate in the opinions and declarations of those who would thus act as mediators between the senate and the people. Let a senator who does not attend the senate, either shew cause of his non-attendance, or submit to an appropriate fine. Let a senator speak in his turn, with all moderation, and let him be thoroughly acquainted with the interests of the people (*senatori qui nec aderit aut causa aut culpa esto—loco senator et modo orato, causas populi teneto.*) By all means avoid violence in politics. Let the greatest authority have the greatest weight in decisions. If any one shall disturb the public harmony, and foment party quarrels, let him be punished as a criminal. To act the intercessor in cases of offence, is the part of a good citizen. Let those who would prosper in their treaties and engagements, duly observe the offices of religion. Let all proclamations be exhibited in the treasury, and published as extensively as possible. Let the public consultations be concentrated in one point at a time, let the people be instructed in the nature of the question, and let all the magistrates and the people be permitted to advise on the subject.

Permit no monopolies, or unfair privileges of one class, at the expense of others. With respect to the capital punishment of any citizen, let it not take place, unless by the adjudication of the high courts of justice, and the ministry of those whom the censors have placed over the popular orders. Let no bribes be given or received, either in soliciting, discharging, or resigning an official situation (*donum ne capiunto, neve danto, neve petenda, neve gerenda, neve gesta potestate*).

If any one shall infringe any of these laws, let him bear the penalty. Let these regulations be committed to the charge of the censors. Let public officers, on their retiring from their posts, give these censors an account of their conduct, but let them not by this means escape from legal prosecution if they have been guilty of corruption.

My code of laws is finished; now, gentlemen, you may retire, and give your votes as you please.

QUINTUS: With what conciseness, my brother, have you delineated the duties and offices of magistrates! But I find the system of laws you would propose for your beau-ideal Commonwealth, very similar to those which prevail in our Roman constitution.

MARCUS: Your observation is very just, my Quintus. It is the very system which Scipio eulogizes in our treatise on the Commonwealth, and which he mainly approves—and it is only by a successive order of magistrates, such as we have described, that the true discipline of the state can be maintained. For you may take for granted that it is the establishment of magistrates, that gives its form to a Commonwealth, and it is exactly by their distribution and subordination, that we must determine the nature of the constitution. Which establishment being very wisely and discreetly settled by our ancestors, I have little or nothing to do with innovation in the laws I propose.

§ 3.13 ATTICUS: Will you be so obliging as to favour us, as you did at my request respecting the ecclesiastical laws, so also now in regard to these magisterial and civil laws,—with the reasons why you prefer the maxims you have stated.

MARCUS: I will do as you desire, my Atticus, and I will explain how far the subject has been illustrated by the disputations of the Greek philosophers, and then prosecute our investigations in jurisprudence.

ATTICUS: I am impatient to hear your dissertation.

MARCUS: I have already stated a large part of the doctrines relating to this enquiry, in the books which I composed respecting the best state of the Commonwealth. In this place, however, we may cite a few of the Greek politicians on the duties and offices of magistrates, which have been treated with considerable subtlety, first by Theophrastus, and next by Dio, the Stoic.

§ 3.14 ATTICUS: A Stoic, say you; were such questions ever discussed by the Stoics?

MARCUS: Certainly not, with the exception of the philosopher I have just cited, and after him Panaetius, whom I take to have been a great man and singularly erudite. Indeed, the ancient Stoics were not so deficient in their speculative dissertations respecting politics and laws, as they were in the practical application of them to the service of the people. From the Platonic school, however, the greatest light was cast over politics and laws. Afterwards, Aristotle illustrated all matters of civil jurisprudence in his elaborate essays, as did also Heraclides of Pontus, another of Plato's disciples. As for Theophrastus, who was instructed by Aristotle, he abounded, as you are aware, in disquisitions of this kind; and Dicaearchus, a disciple of the same master, was by no means deficient in jurisprudential science. After these, Demetrius Phalereus, before mentioned, drew legal learning by his admirable talents from the shades and sequestrations of the schools, into the open daylight of civil life, and gave it a practical point and efficacy, which are of the greatest service in all critical emergencies and conflicts. This combination of legal theory and practice is the more valuable, since we often find that men distinguished in politics are deficient in philosophy, and those celebrated for philosophy are remarkably ignorant in legal affairs. I hardly know where we could find another man of genius, who excels in the theory and practice of jurisprudence, so as to be at once a prince of learning and of political economy. (*Qui vero utraque re excelleret, ut et doctrinae studiis et regenda civitate princeps esset quis facile nunc inveniri protest?*)

ATTICUS: I think I could show you such a man, if I were to point to one of us three; but pray continue your discourse.

MARCUS: These Greek philosophers make it a grand point of enquiry whether a monarch should be appointed in each commonwealth, that is, one chief magistrate, to whom all the rest should be subordinate. This monarchical system, I understand, was very agreeable to our ancestors, even after the expulsion of the Tarquins. But since the monarchy which was at first preferred was changed, not so much through any fault in the monarchy, as through the vices of a monarch, it should seem, that the monarchy itself should still subsist, if one magistrate commanded all the rest, and nothing but the name of king would be lost.

§ 3.16 It was not without reason, therefore, that Theopompus in Lacedaemon, qualified the power of the Spartan kings by the Ephori, or that we Romans qualify the power of our consuls by tribunes. For our consuls are invested with such authority by law, that they command all the other magistrates, except the tribunes, who were created some time after, in order to hinder the abuse of tyranny from being again revived. For the first diminution of the power of the consuls, was the creation of a magistrate who did not hold under them. The next was, when this new magistrate gave his aid not only to other magistrates, but even to private citizens, against any unconstitutional edicts of the consuls.

QUINTUS: Ah, my brother, you speak of a great evil; for since the office of the tribunes of the people was established, the authority of the nobles has declined, and the rule of the mob gained strength.

MARCUS: The case is not quite so bad as you think, my Quintus. For that consular power when unlimited, would not only appear despotic, but even violent to the people, whereas now by a wise and moderate limitation, it diffuses law and justice to all the citizens. Let us now come to the exposition of our legal maxims, before stated; and to pass over that earlier portion whose propriety is almost self–evident, let us notice that maxim which declares, that soldiers should endeavour to return home with unblemished honour.

For to good and innocent men, no prize so valuable as stainless reputation can be derived either from our enemies or our friends. That maxim is also plainly just, that nothing can be baser than for a man to sue for an appointment as ambassador, for any other interest than that of his country. I speak not merely of the conduct of those who would figure as ambassadors and legates and charges d'affairs in order to sequester estates and inheritances in the provinces; for there exist men by no means unfamiliar with this kind of corruption; but I ask, if any thing can be more scandalous than to see senatorial commissioners without commissions, deputies without instructions, or any public business of a patriotic kind? This sort of legation I should have abolished when consul, with the approbation of a full senate, though apparently against the interest of many nobles, had not a certain blundering tribune of the people opposed me. I succeeded, however, in shortening the term of this official abomination, which was before unlimited, and made such appointments merely annual, and thus this scandal still remains, though it has lost its perpetuity.

But now, with your permission, we will wish the provinces good-bye, and once more return to Rome.

ATTICUS: With all my heart, though such a proposition would appear remarkably disagreeable to many gentlemen in the provinces, I could name if I would.

§ 3.19 MARCUS: But if these nameless gentlemen, my Atticus, were content to obey the just laws of their country, they would like nothing better than Rome and their Roman villas; and would hold nothing more laborious and troublesome than their provincial appointments.

The subsequent legal maxim confirms to the tribunes of the people, the power they possess in our commonwealth, on which I need not enlarge.

QUINTUS: I beg your pardon, my brother, but I particularly wish to know your opinion of this power of the tribunes. To me it appears extremely mischievous, at once the child and the parent of endless seditions. If we look back to the origin of the tribunate, we find that it originally sprung from a hubbub of civil disturbances, and that in process of time, a mutinous populace gave it the ascendancy over all magisterial authorities of Rome. After this, being stifled, as one of those monstrous abortions which, by a law of the Twelve Tables, are not suffered to live, it again recovered its existence in a very inexplicable manner, only to become baser and viler than ever. It then committed every kind of atrocity. Its first act was a piece of villainy well worthy of its impious violence, namely, the abrogation of the honours of the senate and patricians. By an infernal system of levelling, it reduced the highest dignities to an equality with the meanest degradations, agitating and confounding all things. When it had thus insulted and violated the gravity of our nobles, it was still as insane and insensate as before.

§ 3.29 Not to mention a Flaminius and others, which you may call antiquated instances, what laws or rights did the tribune Tiberius Gracchus leave to the best and worthiest citizens? And, five years before, did not the tribune Curatius, the basest and foulest of mortals, cast into prison with unheard-of insolence and barbarity, the consuls Brutus and Scipio, patriots of the most effulgent renown? And did not C. Gracchus, another tribune of the people, endeavour to overturn and revolutionize our Commonwealth, by throwing darts and daggers into the forum, in order to excite the citizens to mutual slaughter, as if they were so many gladiators. What shall I say of the crimes of Saturninus and others, whose violences the Commonwealth could scarcely repel without civil war?

§ 3.21 But why should we mention these antique and unfamiliar instances of evil tribunes, when so many occur within our own memory! Who was ever so audacious and so inimical to us, that he ever thought of destroying our state, except through the agency of the tribunes? For when infamous and profligate men found no other means of compassing their evil projects at home or abroad, they endeavoured to rouse the people by the secret instruments of sedition.

Therefore what does us infinite honour, and secures us immortal renown, is the fact, that none of the tribunes could be engaged to appear against us at any bribe, except Clodius, who used the tribunate as a cloak of villainy. As for this monster, what crimes did he not perpetrate—crimes which, without reason or plausible hope, he committed with the fury of some savage beast, maddened with the violence of the brutal mob. I therefore highly approve of the conduct of Sylla in this particular, inasmuch as by his law he rendered the tribunes of the people comparatively impotent for mischief, though he left them the power of doing as much good as they please. As for our friend Pompey, though in most respects I yield him the warmest commendation, I say nothing of his views relating to the power of the tribunes; for here I cannot praise him, and yet I would not censure him.

§ 3.23 MARCUS: You have very clearly unfolded, my Quintus, the defects and abuses of the tribunate; but it is rather unfair thus to state all its faults and omit its merits, and thus to make an enumeration of grievances, a catalogue of blemishes, without any allusion to the redeeming qualities. In this way, you might show up the consulate itself as a very culpable and objectionable institution, if you choose to reckon up all the sins of all the consuls, which I am willing to pass in silence. Even in this power, I confess there are many stains of abuse; but we can never obtain the good we derive from it without some particles of evil. That the authority of the tribunes of the people is too great, none will deny; but the power of the people themselves is much harsher and crueller. It is by having a leader therefore, such as a tribune, that the people behave more temperately than if they had no leader at all. For a leader remembers that he is advancing at his own risk, whereas the violence of the people has no consciousness of its own danger. Sometimes it is suddenly excited, and sometimes suddenly depressed. But what assembly of tribunes is so insane that not one in ten of its members preserves his senses? As to T. Gracchus, you ask, was it not through him that his colleague was dismissed and destroyed? Yes:—but was not this owing to his excessive ambition. What was his reason for this violence, if it were not to get rid of his colleague's power of opposition? In this matter, however, you observe the wisdom of our ancestors. When this office of tribuneship was granted by the senate to the people, wars ceased, seditions were extinguished, and that wholesome liberty was secured, by which meritorious commoners may expect through their labours to rise into the patrician rank, which is one great principle of political welfare. But there were two Gracchi. Yes, and as many more as you will—for though ten tribunes were created, you will find none within our memory very mischievous, though you may discover many who were capricious and immoral. And you will allow me that this high rank is above envy, and that the people no longer enter into perilous contentions concerning their rights.

§ 3.25 Therefore we must acknowledge either that the expulsion of our kings was unnecessary, or that liberty of the people must be guaranteed in fact as well as in profession—and as it is, their liberty is such that they have been obliged to sue the protection of many great patriots, for fear of being oppressed by the senate.

In regard to our private cause, my best and dearest brother, though it fell under the tribunitial power, we had no contention with the tribuneship. For it was not the indignant people that wished to injure us, but a pack of miscreants, whom they let out of prison on purpose to attack us, and reprobate slaves, who live on plunder. Besides this, the alarm which the approach of the troops occasioned, aggravated our disaster. And to confess the truth, we had less to struggle against our private enemies, than with the greivous disorders of the state; and if I had not yielded in some measure to the tempest, my country would not now enjoy the perpetual benefit of my services. And this the event testified,—for what freeman is there, or what bondman worthy of emancipation, to whom our escape is not a subject of congratulation?

If I was so unfortunate, that my efforts on behalf of the Commonwealth did not give universal satisfaction—if the rage of an infuriated mob drove me away by the hurricane of their evil passions; if the tribune Clodius stirred up the populace against me—as Gracchus against Lenas and Saturninus against Metellus,—we bore it, my Quintus, with fortitude, and the consolation of an honest heart. Nor were we less comforted by the counsel of the philosophers of Athens, whose reflections so much alleviate misfortune, than by the example of the illustrious men, who, expelled from their country, were more prompt to desert an ungrateful city, than to remain in a corrupt one.

As to the exception, which you just now made in your panegyric on Pompey, with regard to his treatment of ourselves, you scarcely seem to me sufficiently to recollect, that this great man did what he honestly believed was best in the circumstances of the case, and what he felt necessary at that particular crisis of politics. He knew that a certain share of civic authority must needs be granted to the citizens, which, as the people so ardently desired before they attained it, they would be especially loath to relinquish, when once acquired. It was therefore the part of a wise statesman not to refuse a privilege to the people, which was essentially patriotic, and so highly popular that its denial had been dangerous. If these remarks, my Quintus, shall have modified your opinion, tell me so—for you know, my brother, that in discourses of this kind, an acknowledgement of assent is the very main-spring of the dialogue. (*Scis solere frater in hujus modi sermone, ut transiliri alio possit, admodum dici*).

§ 3.27 ATTICUS: Exactly so.

QUINTUS: I am sorry I can't agree with you respecting Pompey; but this is no reason why you should not go on with our legal maxims.

MARCUS: Then you still persist in your former opinion?

QUINTUS: I do.

ATTICUS: Well, then, my Quintus, we must here agree to differ. But let us, by all means, hear more of your brother's expositions of the maxims of law.

MARCUS: The following maxim allots to all magistrates their auspices and jurisdictions. Their jurisdictions, I say, in such a manner that there should still be a supreme court of justice, to which appeals may be made by the people. And the auspices, because they furnish a plausible method of adjourning useless or mischievous assemblies. For in this way it has often happened that the gods have suppressed by means of auspices the unjust impetuosity of the mob.

Another legal maxim is this,—Let the senate be composed of those who have exercised magistracies. This provision is evidently popular, since it permits none to arrive at high authority without the approbation of the people, leaving the ipse dixit of the censors of little effect. But lest this should seem to favour democratic ascendancy, another provision immediately follows, by which the authority of the senate is confirmed.

It is thus expressed: Let the decrees of the senate have the force of laws. For if it so happen that the senate becomes master of public politics, and all men defend its decrees; and if the inferior orders agree that the Commonwealth shall be governed by this superior order, there will arise from this amalgamation of rights, namely, the authority of the senate and the power of the people, the modified and harmonic kind of constitution which I have so highly extolled.

This will be especially the case, if the following legal maxim be observed: "Let the senatorial order be free from corruption, and let it be a pattern to others."

QUINTUS: This is an admirable maxim, my brother. It is of the utmost importance that this order be free from corruption; but a censor would have enough to do to enforce such a regulation.

ATTICUS: He would indeed, and although the senatorial order is devoted to your interests, my Marcus, and retains a most grateful memorial of your consulship, I would, with your permission, suggest, that not only all censors, but all judges might well grow weary of so painful a task.

MARCUS: I am sadly afraid of it, my Atticus; but let us leave this question for the present, for our business is not so much with the senate of today, or our contemporary statesmen, as with future politicians, if any of them shall be complaisant enough to attend to our legal maxims. If such a law were carried, that the senator should be exempt from all corruption, the vicious candidate would not dare to present himself in parliamentary elections. An event, indeed most devoutly to be wished, but most difficultly to be realized, unless perhaps by a certain education and discipline, on which we might speak more at large, if time and occasion permitted.

§ 3.30 ATTICUS: Why, you can't have a better occasion than the present, since you are now laying down a system of laws. And as to time, the length of this summer holiday will ensure you a hearing. But if you choose to omit this topic now, I shall not forget to demand your views on education and discipline on the first opportunity.

MARCUS: I cannot refuse, my Atticus, to grant any request that comes from you. I will therefore enlarge a little on this legal maxim before cited, let the senator be a pattern to others. If this is observed, all will go well. For as a whole city is infected by the licentious passions and vices of great men, so it is often reformed by their virtue and moderation. L. Lucullus, a man of the first rank, being rallied for the magnificence of his seat at Tusculum, is said to have made the following extremely suitable answer—that he had two neighbours, the greater of whom was only a Roman knight, and the other, the son of one who had been once a slave; and as each of them had magnificent villas, that could not be thought extravagance in himself, a consul, which was lawful for those of inferior rank. Alas! Lucullus; you little thought that it was you that gave rise to their ambition. Were it not for your example, such an action in them would have been looked on as criminal. Who could bear that people of this sort should have their villas crowded with statues and pictures, relating either to public, or what is more, to sacred and religious subjects? Who would not join in demolishing the monuments of their vanity and pride, if those who ought to exert themselves on such occasions were not guilty of the same extravagance? For the mischief immediately attending the vices of the great, though that must be allowed to be very considerable, is but small compared with the ill consequences which arise from the multitude of those who will certainly follow their example.

Would you but look into the history of former ages, you might plainly see that the manners of the people were always regulated by those of the leading men of a state; and that whatever change took place in the latter, the same always happened in the former.

§ 3.32 Now this observation is much more certain than that of Plato, who pretends that a change in the songs of musicians is able to alter the manners of a nation—whereas my opinion is, that the manners of mankind change with those of their superiors. Hence, great men of a vicious life are doubly pernicious to the state, as being not only guilty of immoral practices themselves, but likewise of spreading them far and wide among their fellow-citizens. The mischief they do, is owing not only to their being debauched themselves, but also to their debauching a crowd of their foolish imitators. In a word, they do more harm by their example than by the crimes they commit.

This maxim, though we would wish to extend its influence to the whole body of senators, would be of great service, even if it were observed by a few of them. For even a few noblemen, aye, even a very few, illustrious in fame and fortune, may correct the morals or manners of the state, or cast them into grievous corruptions. But we have said enough on this topic, which we discussed at large in our treatise on the Commonwealth. Let us therefore proceed.

§ 3.33 The next legal maxim treats of suffrages and votes, which, as I have said, should be known for the nobles, and free for the people (*nota optimatibus, populo libera*).

ATTICUS: I have given much attention to this maxim, but I do not well understand its spirit or its sense.

MARCUS: I confess, my Atticus, we have now to treat on a very difficult question, and one already much discussed,—that question is, whether, in case of suffrages at the election of magistrates, or in the formation of laws, or in the judgment of criminals, the votes should be given openly by poll or secretly by ballot.

QUINTUS: Is it indeed a doubtful question? I fear we shall again differ in opinion.

MARCUS: I do not think so, my Quintus, for here I hold that doctrine, which I know you always maintained, that in giving suffrages and votes, nothing can be better than an open viva voce declaration, (nihil ut fuerit in suffragiis voce melius).—But let us examine how far it is attainable.

§ 3.34 QUINTUS: With your permission, my brother, I should say that the distinction you take between the propriety and the practicability of any measure, is fraught with mischief to the inexperienced. It is often hurtful to the state, when a regulation is said to be true and proper in itself, but at the same time, that it cannot be obtained, because it cannot be carried without opposing the people. Now, I say, the people are to be opposed whenever they act amiss, and it is better for patriotic lawyers to suffer in a good cause, than yield to a bad one. Now, who does not perceive that all authority is taken away from our nobility and gentry by the present Roman law of balloting (*Quis autem non sensit auctoritatem omnem optimatium tabellariam legem abstulisse*). A law which the people, when free, never desired, but which they claimed when oppressed by the domination and power of certain aristocrats. It is no wonder, therefore, that the system of open polling and viva voce votes, presents us with more severe judgments against the grandees, than the present plan of ballots. Therefore it had been far better te restrain the excessive influence of the great for unjustifiable objects in elective suffrages, than to give the people a mask and veil, by which they may keep the more honourable citizens in ignorance of their individual sentiments, and thus make the ballot a mere cover for corrupt and hypocritical votes. (*Quamobrem suffragandi nimia libido in non bonis causis eripienda fuit potentibus, non latebra dando populo in quâ bonis ignorantibus quid quisque sentiret tabella vitiorum occultaret suffragium.*)

For this reason, it is that no good man was ever a proposer or supporter of the system of ballotting. (Itaque isti rationi neque lator quisquam est inventus neque auctor unquam bonus). There are four laws of ballots: the first, concerning the election of magistrates, was proposed by a certain Gabinius, an unknown and sordid agitator. The second, respecting the adjudications of the people, was proposed two years afterwards by Cassius, who was a nobleman,—but with his family's permission, I venture to say, a nobleman opposed to all goodness, driven to and fro by the idlest rumours of the populace. The third, regarding the ratification or nullification of laws, was carried by Carbo, a seditious and profligate citizen, whose return to the better classes of society never secured him the approbation of the aristocracy.

§ 3.36 There remained only the crime of treason, which Cassius himself excepted, in the judgment of which, open viva voce votes were permitted. But Caelius soon after thought proper to give traitors also the chance of the ballot, and manifested as long as he lived, that, provided he could oppress Popilius, he cared little or nothing for the injury of the state. Our grandfather, a man of singular virtue in this town Arpinum, as long as he lived opposed Gratidius, whose sister, our grandmother, he had married. And, therefore, when Gratidius wanted to introduce the law of ballot here, he roused as many waves in our family circle as his son Marius afterwards stirred up in the Aegean sea. To such a length did the quarrel proceed, that the consul Scaurus, informed of what past, made this remark to our grandfather: Would to heaven, Cicero, that a man of your courage and honour, had better loved to live in the capital of our Commonwealth, than to retire into a country villa.

§ 3.37 Therefore, since our design is not so much to state the Roman laws now in force, but in order to form a more perfect code of jurisprudence, both to revive those good laws that have become obsolete, and to propose new regulations, suitable to the present conditions of society, I think we are by no means bound to limit ourselves by the caprice of the populace, who cry out for ballot. I conceive you are entitled to take higher ground; for in your treatise on the Commonwealth, your Scipio does not hesitate to condemn the law of Cassius as injudicious, whoever was its author. If you take away the law of ballot you will do still better. For in truth I don't like it at all, nor does our friend Atticus much admire it, if I may judge by his countenance.

ATTICUS: For me, I never admired any thing that pleases the mob, and I regard the best state of the Commonwealth, to be that which your brother, when consul, promoted, wherein the power of the aristocracy prevailed over that of the populace. (*Mihi vero nihi lun quam populare placuit, eamque optimam Rempublicam esse duco, quam hic consul constituerat quae sit in potestate optimorum.*)

MARCUS: I see, gentlemen, you would repeal my law respecting suffrages, without any ballot whatsoever. For myself, though I have sufficiently justified in my Commonwealth the line of conduct assumed by Scipio, yet I would not practically go quite so far as he.

It is only under the authority of the nobles, which good men will obey, that I concede the right of voting to the people. For these are the very words of my law respecting elections. Let the votes be notorious to the nobles, and free to the people. (*Optimatibus nota plebi libera sunto*). Which legal maxim contains this doctrine, that all those laws should be abrogated which have been so contrived as in any way to mask or hide a suffrage; such as those which hinder full inspection of any ballot, or examination and appeal thereupon, and that law of Marius, which makes the passages to the balloting boxes so narrow, should be likewise abolished. (*Quae lex hanc sententiam continet ut omnes leges tollat quae postea latae sunt, quæ tegunt omni ratione suffragium ne quis inspiciat tabellam ne roget ne appellat. Pontes lex maria fecit angustos*).

If these rules are opposed, as they generally are, to the ambitious, they are worthy our approval. If the laws indeed could but hinder intrigues, then the people might be allowed the ballot as a vindicator of liberty, provided it were so laid open and freely exposed to all honourable and worthy citizens, that their authority might be blended with this popular privilege, thus leaving the people the power of expressing their deference for the aristocracy. But why is it, Quintus, as you just now observed, that there were more condemnations past by the open suffrages of the poll, than by the silent secret votes of the ballot? We should explain the anomoly thus. The people are extremely fond of licence; do but save appearances in this respect, and they will abandon their influence to authority or favour. As to the largesses and bribes which are given to obtain corrupt suffrages, do you not see if we could but get rid of bribery, the characters and counsels of the best men would carry the votes? By our legal maxim, therefore, the appearance of liberty is conceded, but as the superintendence of the aristocracy is still retained, the cause of contention is banished.

§ 3.40 The following legal maxim relates to those magistrates, whose right it is to treat with the senate and the people, and to reconcile their interests as far as possible.

The next regulation appears to me very notable and important:—viz. that whenever there is any such compromise between the senate and the people, the utmost moderation should be observed, and the speeches on both sides be made with that modesty and fairness, which tend to allay passions and mitigate asperities. Every mob orator, modifies and moulds not merely the opinions and desires, but the very features of his audience. It is not so in the senate, however; for the senator should not permit himself to imitate the fashion of the mob orator, but will rather endeavour to speak with absolute decorum and propriety.

We therefore require three duties from the senator. First, that his attendance in the senate be regular; for the multitude of senators lends weight to the arguments of policy.—Secondly, that he should speak in his turn, that is, when his counsel is demanded. Thirdly.—That he should speak concisely, lest he should become infinitely wearisome; for brevity in parliamentary oratory, and all kinds of oratory, is the best recommendation of a speech.

Lengthy speeches therefore are never seasonable, except when the senate is precipitating some rash measure, as it does far too often, through the ambition and corruption of its members. In such a case, it may be desirable for a speaker, not being duly seconded by another representative, to occupy a whole day. The same privilege may be allowed where the subject of debate is so important as to demand all the copiousness of the orator, both hortatory and explanatory, in which our own Cato is remarkably distinguished.

§ 3.41 The ensuing legal maxim ordains that magistrates be very studious of the interests of the people. For it is necessary for a senator to be acquainted with politics in general, and this is a science of the greatest importance to the Commonwealth; since it comprehends its military affairs, its commercial statistics and revenue, its foreign alliances, its colonies and stipendiaries. He should be familiar with their regulations, their resources, and their engagements; their customs and modes of life. You therefore see that the science of politics taxes every power of intellect and memory, in order to acquire and maintain that elaborate information, without which no one can be called an accomplished senator.

Then follows a legal maxim, which relates to the public deliberations of the people, in which it is especially enjoined hat all violence be avoided (*vis abesto*). For nothing is more destructive in states, nothing more contrary to law and right, nothing less civil and humane, than to carry any thing by violence and agitation in a sound and constitutional government.

The next maxim relates to the office of comptrollers,—which is an admirable institution, since it is better that a good measure be sometimes impeded than a bad one carried.

When I say, in all cases of fraud, it is necessary to go before a pleader, I follow the opinion of Crassus, one of our wisest men, whose counsel was adopted by the senate, which decreed when the consul Claudius reported Carbo's sedition, that they could not take cognizance of sedition, except through the medium of an official pleader, who should lay the case before the people. Since it was allowable for him who made a proposition to abandon it as soon as it began to occasion disturbance; and if he persisted, when he could do no good, he would be held accessory to a breach of the peace, which we would punish severely.

Then follows that maxim, which states, that he who acts as a comptroller of civil abuses, shall be considered as a good citizen. And who would not promote the interests of the Commonwealth, with all his energy, when stimulated by the hope of acquiring a character so glorious?

Next, succeed certain regulations, which we likewise find in the public institutions and laws—that auspices be observed, and augurs obeyed. It is the duty of a good augur to show himself in the critical periods of the Commonwealth, as Jupiter's minister and prophet; since those to whom he has entrusted the auspices are his instruments of revelation; and he has revealed his celestial influences to them, in order that they may succour the state in her hour of danger and necessity.

Then follows a provision respecting the promulgation of laws, that they ought to be proposed distinctly in their successive counts and clauses, and that the remonstrances and objections not of the magistrates only, but of private individuals, should be duly weighed.

After this, we find two excellent laws selected from the Twelve Tables. One of these forbids unfair privileges and partialities: the other will not permit sentence of death to he past on any citizen except in the high courts of justice. You may think it odd that such decisions were not left to seditious tribunes of the people; but our ancestors provided for posterity, that laws should not be enacted in favour of particular individuals, for that is what we call privilege than which nothing can be more inequitable. Since it is most important that every law should be equally published and enjoined to all, they refused to sanction any particular enactments which were not openly proposed in the assembled commons, (centuriatis comitiis). For when the people are summoned by rank, order, and age, they use much more consideration in giving their suffrages, than when they are promiscuously convoked by tribes.

§ 3.45 It was therefore very truly observed in my own particular cause, by L. Cotta, a man of vast genius and consummate prudence, that no sentence was legally pronounced against us, since the only body of commons that prosecuted us was an armed mob of slaves. Such comitia tributa could neither pass capital sentence nor special adjudications (*privilegia*). There was therefore no need of a law for my recal, since the sentence of my banishment was wholly illegal. But it appeared to you and other illustrious men more proper, seeing these slaves and vagabonds persisted in declaring they had justly condemned me, to manifest as openly as possible what all Italy thought on the subject.

Next follow those laws which relate to pecuniary bribes and intrigues. And since these cannot be so well chastised by censures as by penalties, it is added, let all such abuses be visited with penalty and punishment, so that every one be duly punished for this disgraceful corruption: the avaricious by fines, and the ambitious by ignominy.

The last laws we have cited, are not in use among us, though very necessary to the state. We have no proper registration of laws (*custodiam legum*). Our laws, therefore, are such as the apparitors declare them to be, and we are forced to take the word of their copyists as our security. We want some public legal registry, in which our laws may lie open to the notice of the people. The Greeks are more careful than ourselves in this matter, as they have instituted legal registrars, whom they call nomophylaces. Their office is not only to preserve the original copies of the laws, as was the custom among our ancestors, but also to summon back to the law, observing the conduct of the citizens.

§ 3.47 This case we might entrust to the censors, since we wish to maintain their function in the state. It is likewise to the censors, according to our legal maxim, that those who retire from magisterial offices should unfold and explain their proceedings when in office, in order to enable the censors to report them fairly. There existed a very similar institution in Greece, where public examiners were directed to inspect official accounts. But these examiners could never have much weight unless their functions were voluntary and honorary. It is therefore better to state the case, and explain the accounts to the censors. And in case of error, leave the whole suit to the law, the plaintiff, and the judge. But I presume we have sufficiently discussed the offices and duties of magistrates, unless you demand further information on any point.

ATTICUS: Why—if we held our peace, the very subject itself would admonish you what you ought further to say.

§ 3.48 MARCUS: On my honour, Atticus, I suppose you want me, since I have treated of judges, next to treat of judgments.

ATTICUS: What then, do you think nothing remains to be said on the rights of the Romans, which you proposed to investigate?

MARCUS: What would you have me say on such a topic?

ATTICUS: I think you should treat of those regulations, which all who live in our Commonwealth ought to understand. For as you remarked just now, a knowledge of our laws is too much confined to their copyists; and I observe that many of our magistrates are so ignorant of their own laws, that they know no more about them than their clerks choose to tell them. Since therefore, when you had explained the laws of religion, you went on to treat of the observance of religious obligations; so as you have described the laws of our magistrates, you should elucidate their jurisdictions and their judgments.

§ 3.49 MARCUS: Well, my Atticus, I will endeavour to do so, as briefly as I can. For your father's friend M. Junius, addressed to him an extensive treatise on this subject, which, in my opinion, is extremely well and ingeniously written. Of this book, we shall freely avail ourselves. When indeed we discussed the law of nature, we drew from our own souls, and delivered our own opinions; but if we go on to consider the civil rights of the Romans, we will accumulate all the authorities we can procure from the traditions and records of our predecessors.

ATTICUS: Such, indeed, appears to me the right method of proceeding, and I shall listen with pleasure to all you may choose to say on these topics.

§ 5.1 FRAGMENTS.

As one and the same universal nature unites and corroborates all the parts of the world, so did she unite into one harmonious family all mankind. But men through their depravity disagreed and quarrelled, not recollecting that they are all consanguineous and akin, and equally subject to the same paternal providence. If this fact, indeed, were but kept in mind, all men might live the amiable life of the gods.

It was a very bold and hazardous measure of the Greek government to consecrate the images of Love and Cupid in the public theatres.

Let us congratulate ourselves, since death gives us something better than we enjoy in life, and not a worse condition of things. For that immortality may truly be termed divine, wherein the mind flourishes, emancipated from the body; and being delivered from sensuality, is free from evil.

For more enlightening reads, visit maximapress.com.

Printed in Dunstable, United Kingdom

64368266R00102